Praise for
Breaking *into* Blossom

"It goes without saying that Luke Hankins and Nomi Stone have curated a star-studded anthology of writers—from Ilya Kaminsky to C.D. Wright and Ross Gay—who cultivate an aura of surprise and wonder as their poems draw to a close. But to stop there would be to greatly underestimate Hankins's and Stone's powers as editors. What I find so compelling about this anthology—in addition to the masterful craft of the writers gathered here—is the project's ethical and philosophical underpinnings. Here, Hankins and Stone set forth an ethics of poetic closure, as well as a detailed and practical taxonomy of all the myriad ways a poem can 'break into blossom.' Hankins and Stone reveal a poem's aesthetics as being inextricable from its ethics, and this nuance makes for an incredible teaching tool. This volume is an achievement, a beacon, and a masterclass. Bravo!"

—KRISTINA MARIE DARLING, author of *Look To Your Left: A Feminist Poetics of Spectacle* and *Daylight Has Already Come: Poems*

"Editors Luke Hankins and Nomi Stone have assembled an extraordinary anthology. The editors build an ambitious taxonomy allowing for a variety of starting points to connect with the endings of poems. This is an anthology that empowers us to discover poetry in the world around us."

—RUBEN QUESADA, author of *Brutal Companion*

Breaking *into* Blossom

Breaking *into* Blossom

Poems with Extraordinary Endings

Edited By
Luke Hankins & Nomi Stone

TRP: The University Press of SHSU
Huntsville, Texas 77341

Library of Congress Cataloging-in-Publication Data
Names: Hankins, Luke, 1984- editor. | Stone, Nomi, editor.
Title: Breaking into blossom : poems with extraordinary endings / edited by Luke Hankins & Nomi Stone.
Description: First edition. | Huntsville, Texas : TRP: The University Press of SHSU, 2026. | Includes bibliographical references.
Identifiers: LCCN 2025018756 (print) | LCCN 2025018757 (ebook) | ISBN 9781680034387 (trade paperback) | ISBN 9781680034394 (ebook)
Subjects: LCSH: Poetry, Modern--20th century. | Poetry, Modern--21st century. | Epiphanies--Poetry. | LCGFT: Poetry.
Classification: LCC PN6101 .B735 2025 (print) | LCC PN6101 (ebook) | DDC 821/.9108--dc23/eng/20250615
LC record available at https://lccn.loc.gov/2025018756
LC ebook record available at https://lccn.loc.gov/2025018757

FIRST EDITION

Cover design by Cody Gates, Happenstance Type-O-Rama
Interior design by Maureen Forys, Happenstance Type-O-Rama

Printed and bound in the United States of America
First Edition Copyright: 2026

TRP: The University Press of SHSU
Huntsville, Texas 77341
texasreviewpress.org

Contents

Introduction

Aesthetics and Ethics in Poetic Closure

Luke Hankins & Nomi Stone

This anthology takes us to the end of the poem—and "out of the poem's tunnel of words," as Marianne Boruch puts it, where we might suddenly be "blinking slightly, released from some dark, eyes adjusting, what was ordinary seen differently now. Or not."[1]

W. H. Auden famously said, paraphrasing Paul Valéry, "A poem is never finished; it is only abandoned."[2] This statement applies to more than simply the ending of the poem, of course, but it certainly evokes the questions of where and how to end a poem. In this anthology, we aim to present poems that enact remarkable answers to these questions. We have no ambition to catalog every possible type of poem ending, but rather to present poems whose endings we find particularly impactful, and to think together in this introductory essay about the characteristics of these—in our view—extraordinary endings.

We decided to focus on recent and contemporary poems. Since all anthologies have to have limits of some sort, we've selected work by poets who were born in or after 1927[3], the birth year of James Wright, from whom we gleaned our title.

From the late 20th century to today, critics and poets have often expressed suspicion of "neat" endings that provide a type of closure that lends itself to a single interpretation rather

---

[1] Marianne Boruch, "The End Inside It," *New England Review* 33.2 (2012), https://www.nereview.com/ner-33-2the-end-inside-it-by-marianne-boruch/.

[2] See W. H. Auden, "Author's Forewords," in *W. H. Auden: Collected Poems*, ed. Edward Mendelson (New York: Vintage, 2007), xxx. Valéry's original statement is, "A work is never completed except by some accident such as weariness, satisfaction, the need to deliver, or death: for, in relation to who or what is making it, it can only be one stage in a series of inner transformations" (in "Recollection" from *Collected Works Vol. 1.* Trans. David Paul. Princeton, NJ: Princeton University Press, 2016).

[3] With one exception: Osip Mandlestom (trans. Christian Wiman), whose poem "And I Was Alive" offers such an excellent example of a paradoxical ending (see p. 157).

than ambiguity or meaning co-created between the text and the reader. Jacob Edmond observes that "the literary-critical climate of recent decades has overwhelmingly favored openness over closure,"[4] and Rachel Cole notes that "In the last decade of the twentieth century, [...] the lyric attracted considerable critical hostility, in large part because of its association with closure."[5] Alina Ștefănescu expresses a desire for "an ending that doesn't need to be neat and sweetly-knotted. The poem may end in an entire new opening...."[6] Such statements call into question how our expectations of poetic and psychological completeness influence the tendency to valorize "neat" endings. In such discussions, epiphany—seen as epitomizing closure—often comes under scrutiny as a feature of many celebrated poems.

An ending that offers satisfaction in one respect—formal completion, say, or aural resonance—does not always provide a "closed" singular meaning or epiphanic certainty, however.[7] In a recent lecture, Carl Phillips said that he writes until he is surprised by the poem, and that he doesn't "write past the surprise."[8] He explicitly contrasted this approach to the way many poems in the Western tradition have operated over the centuries, in that they seek a resolution or closure that extends past or incorporates a surprise that has occurred in order to find a resting place, an equilibrium, poetic and psychological completeness. Phillips's statement implies that epiphany—if we can read "surprise" as the equivalent of epiphany—is not always the same thing as a "neat ending," and that epiphany can function to disorient or to challenge psychological or even formal equilibrium. Perhaps critics have too often equated epiphany and certainty.

---

[4] Jacob Edmond, "The Closures of the Open Text: Lyn Hejinian's 'Paradise Found.'" *Contemporary Literature*, 50.2 (2009), 240–272.

[5] Rachel Cole, "Rethinking the Value of Lyric Closure: Giorgio Agamben, Wallace Stevens, and the Ethics of Satisfaction." *PMLA*, 126.2 (2011), 383–97.

[6] Alina Ștefănescu. "Interview with Alina Ștefănescu." *Mentor & Muse*. Accessed May 28, 2024. https://mentorandmuse.net/alina-stefanescu/.

[7] By "open," we mean to suggest endings that are more uncertain, more receptive to interpretation by the reader, and more multiple in their possible meanings. By "closed," we mean poems that narrow into a clearer single interpretation, via content, craft choices, and/or formal conventions. We use these terms loosely, following their definition by Lyn Hejinian in "The Rejection of Closure" (and without allying ourselves singularly with a position).However, unlike literary theory, creative writing generally doesn't demand that we choose to privilege the formal properties of a poem (and the intent of its maker) *or* the experience of the reader as the singular key element. Rather, we instead consider poems along a spectrum, where authorial intentions, reader experiences, *and* formal properties co-produce endings which are variably more certain or uncertain. Thank you to Charles Hatfield, Shilyh Warren, and Matthew Baker for conversations on these topics.

[8] Carl Phillips, The Harwood-Cole Literary Lecture, Warren Wilson College. Feb. 25, 2024.

Lawrence Raab says, "The problem—and the great pleasure—of reading poems, and of writing them, is how to remain faithful to the truth of uncertainty."[9] Even closing statements that sound as if the poem or its speaker has arrived at a conclusion or a solidified idea are often far from imparting an unambiguous meaning to the reader. Poetic epiphanies can record the discovery of the speaker's uncertainty or limitation rather than certainty or authority.

James Wright's famous poem "Lying in a Hammock at William Duffy's Farm in Pine Island, Minnesota" provides an interesting example of both of these characteristics. The broad structure of the poem is a detailed sensory observation of the speaker's surroundings, followed by a single declarative sentence that likely at first strikes the reader as a non-sequitur: "I have wasted my life."[10] The speaker has arrived at this epiphany, seemingly, through quiet consideration of his rural surroundings. The statement itself sounds absolute, certain, unambiguous. But while it may be unambiguous for the poem's speaker, the reader is left with a multiplicity of possible meanings. In what sense has the speaker wasted his life, and why does this realization come to him here, in this particular setting? Does he regret having spent his life far from the natural world, or from the manual labor that would be necessary on the farm? Or perhaps he feels that he's kept himself too busy and distracted to appreciate the glorious details of the world around him, like he's doing now in the hammock. But it could be quite the reverse: What if he's always been prone to lazy daydreaming, and he catches himself doing that yet again? Or maybe he realizes he's gathering material to turn into art—into the poem itself—and feels that he hasn't devoted himself adequately to artistic pursuits. All of these possibilities and more simultaneously turn in the reader's mind. This is no "closed" text, despite the tonal certainty of its final declaration. And yet the conclusive sound of the declaration offers one kind of satisfaction to the reader, and the poem imparts a feeling of completion. In this way, conclusion and inconclusiveness occur simultaneously. As to the speaker's authority, the fact that he is admitting his perceived failure to himself—and the poem is admitting it to the reader—positions him as someone who has fallen short in his own estimation. This epiphany has the potential to be a humbling experience for the speaker.

Another famous poem of Wright's, "A Blessing" (from which we gleaned the title for this anthology), has an epiphanic ending that might be read as more "closed" than "Lying in a Hammock…." The meaning, for the speaker, of the final annotative line—a line which

[9] "Uncertain Clarity: Some Ways Poems End," *Mentor and Muse,* https://mentorandmuse.net/lawrence-raab/.

[10] James Wright, "Lying in a Hammock at William Duffy's Farm in Pine Island, Minnesota," in *Collected Poems* (Middletown, CT: Wesleyan University Press, 1971), 114.

breaks against the syntax, according to James Longenbach—is likely more obvious to most readers than the ending of "Lying in a Hammock. . . ." The poem begins with a measured pace and "parsing lines"[11] that break following the natural syntax as the poet approaches a pair of ponies. As he zooms in, an increasing generosity and tenderness accrue, rising in intensity toward the middle of the poem as Wright positions three short sentences on a single line, and then culminates in the final surprising break: "Suddenly I realize / That if I stepped out of my body I would break / Into blossom."[12] The annotative linebreak steers the reader into a moment of doubleness and incandescence, where we first break and then revise our breaking, adding to it a blossoming.

But, quite ironically, it turns out that the poem which was the very catalyst for this anthology has also prompted a bifurcation in this essay—a pivot to two voices rather than one, to wrestle with different ways of seeing the poetic ending.

NS: I do wonder if these Wright poems in some way implicitly posit these experiences as universal, actually, and also white and male. While it may be that the poet is describing his own subjective feeling of transport, the craft choices here shepherd us into Wright's experience of anguish and ecstasy as if this is how one must or should feel amidst a pastoral encounter like this.

LH: I find that argument hard to follow. Should we expect a poet not to write from their own subject position? Does doing so imply that they believe that everyone will identify with their experience? Isn't art of all kinds predicated on some degree of universality in the human experience, but also the understanding that not all work will appeal equally to everyone, that not everyone will identify with it?

I'd say that Wright's poem invites us in and attempts to allow us into a vicarious experience that might strike us as miraculously familiar. The poem invites us to participate. It doesn't coerce us—indeed, it can't. Empathy, vicarious experience...these are the foundations of literature and art, in my view.

Aren't we all writing in the hope that a handful of people somewhere, sometime, will be deeply impacted by our work, rather than out of some presumption of universal appeal? Is a white, male poet writing from his subject position inherently excluding any reader, including readers of other gender identities and ethnicities?

---

[11] James Longenbach, *The Resistance to Poetry* (Chicago: University of Chicago Press, 2004), 19. See also Longenbach, *The Art of the Poetic Line* (Minneapolis: Graywolf Press, 2007).

[12] James Wright, "A Blessing," in *Collected Poems* (Middletown, CT: Wesleyan University Press, 1971), 135.

NS: To be honest, I'm suspicious of empathy. What experiences are readers being recruited into? And what experiences are readers imagining they are consuming from the inside? More generally, I think what I'm still wrestling with is the experience of the narrative-lyric epiphanic poem. Listen: I personally have always been seduced by epiphanies, which is why I'm asking myself to wrestle more with their structure. We concur that epiphanies don't need to be conclusive or tidy stamps on experience—or what Charles Baxter calls "a brilliant visionary stop-time moment."[13] But I still think we have to slow down with the implications of Lyn Hejinian's provocation that the epiphanic mode at its worst can even be "coercive... with its smug pretension to universality and its tendency to cast the poet as guardian to Truth."[14] This feels worrisome when the great questions are so frequently answered in this manner by a canon of white male speakers.

Quite right: everyone can and should only write from their own subject position (the complexities of persona poems aside, they are still mediated by the self). But I wonder if some of these very famous poems (often written by white men), with their more linear crescendos, structurally and tacitly assume they will chime with everyone? Such poems circulate as if they are for everyone and meant to bless everyone. And sometimes with craft, they work to corral us into those endings. Perhaps it's true that Wright's "Lying in a Hammock..." allows for a more open ending, but I found Aditi Machado's critique of this poem so compelling, as well, questioning Wright as being "far too assured of his ability to wield language-as-tool, to direct his own consciousness."[15] And as for "A Blessing," a poem I had read at my own wedding, a poem I have loved for years, I think it is perhaps easier to mark as an excellent ending the swelling orchestra of a body "breaking / Into blossom"—that tandem joy and anguish—than other kinds of poems. In *The End*, Machado retorts, "To compose a ten-line poem, say, with a good first and a devastating last line—it doesn't move me. Though, of course, poems do have last lines and sometimes the last line devastates. But that's not (really) the (only) end of a poem. The poem's end is to endure."[16]

So what makes a poem endure? I'm increasingly convinced by another genealogy of conversation on this topic, a genealogy that is a bit suspicious of the lyric poem. As someone who is passionate about reading and writing so-called lyric poems, these cautions feel all the more urgent to me. Hejinian asks us to consider rejecting tidier forms of closure, offering a counter-model where the

---

[13] Charles Baxter, "Against Epiphanies," in *Burning Down the House* (Saint Paul, MN: Graywolf Press, 1997), 66.

[14] Lyn Hejinian, "The Rejection of Closure," in *The Language of Inquiry* (Berkeley: University of California Press, 2000), 41.

[15] Aditi Machado, *The End* (New York: Ugly Duckling Presse, 2020), 11.

[16] Ibid., 8.

poem is considered "as if it were a mind."[17] Both the mind and the poem keep going. For example, she suggests we not make one event or moment carry all the meaning. To this end, a craft tool like repetition in a poem allows us to shift our initial readings, in fact "postpon[ing] completion of the thought indefinitely." This is really seductive to me as a counter-model to an epiphanic ending with singular pyrotechnics.

I'm thinking of francine j. harris's poem, "enough food and a mom," which proposes a very different answer to the work of ending—an ending that endures for me for other reasons. In the poem, harris denatures lexical units—in this case, the words "mom" and "dad"—to, in my opinion, make them more capacious and able to house other possibilities. The words "mom" and "dad" are a sort of ideal, normative unit that we are all supposed to understand as being the origin of a family. Through the course of the poem, she evacuates them of their previous content and remakes them, for example: "She thinks she could make her own insulin. to keep from going into dad" and "The mom is a yard of blackening petals."[18] Over the course of the poem, she turns "mom" and "dad" into states of being, emotional possibilities and voids, ghosts, and even smells. The final turn has long endured for me, and it lands so resoundingly because I have been swept into the architecture, the form, the poet has created, the mutable wells of language which she has activated. In the last line, she writes, "I mom of you. I mom of you a lot."[19] In this moment, "mom" turns into a verb and a way that the speaker herself might become other—a principle of transformation. For me, the form of the poem is doing key work all on its own, both proposing and allowing me to imagine a kind of otherwise, to become new through syntax and structure. But I also feel in some way tended by the speaker in my reseeing, as if those meanings are being released incrementally, and I am able to participate in them. Rather than being severed and tumble at the linebreak with Wright as we "break / Into blossom," we have to move forward and backward within the poem, in the puzzle of form and syntax that harris has made, to house an ache.

I guess I'm answering your questions in a meandering way, but I agree that for me, to write a poem is to hope that it will resonate somewhere for someone, and I certainly don't fantasize about universal appeal. I don't think that exists. In fact, I feel suspicious about universalism at all, or at least the paradoxical content of many universals as they are currently posited, things like "beauty" or "freedom." I guess my longing is to create a realm here in this anthology with as many different kinds of poems with different aesthetics and poetics and subject positions and possible resonances for different readers, and different kinds of endings (both those that embrace and those that refuse

---

[17] Hejinian, 80.

[18] francine j. harris, "enough food and a mom" in *Play Dead* (New Gloucester, ME: Alice James Books, 2016), 83.

[19] Ibid.

the structure of epiphany) as we can: endings that crescendo to a height, endings that taper down, endings that seem to end flatly; endings that end after resisting an ending, endings that invert precedent, endings that work through a perceptual mistake; endings that catapult back to the reader, endings that seem to simply not end, endings that newly activate a language world. Some of these endings might provide Frost's "momentary stay against confusion."[20] Others linger in the tangle and refuse satisfaction or closure, as so often does the world.

LH: I think there are many poems in the canon that fall into the presumption that Hejinian identifies—the end of Keats's "Ode on a Grecian Urn," for instance: "'Beauty is truth, truth beauty,'—that is all / Ye know on earth, and all ye need to know."[21] A simple way of saying it is that these poems overly simplify and are didactic or "preachy." My worry, though, is that what Hejinian calls coercive pretension gets applied to epiphany itself, rather than to particular instances of it. She doesn't identify a single negative example in her essay, so it comes off as a blanket prohibition against epiphany and endings whose meanings are relatively singular and clear (i.e., "closed"). There's an irony, to me, in her sweeping implication that epiphany and clear meaning themselves are unethical or at fault. To me, *that* is a presumption and a dismissal of nuance. As we've already noted, there are all sorts of epiphanies, and all sorts of ways of writing them.

You quoted from Frost's essay "The Figure a Poem Makes"—an essay I love. Frost writes that a poem "ends in a clarification of life—not necessarily a great clarification, such as sects and cults are founded on, but in a momentary stay against confusion."[22] Such an epiphany is not troublesome to me, but rather welcome—an epiphany that is humble, that doesn't seek to break out of its own subjectivity, allowing the reader to determine how closely they identify with it. Obvious exceptions would be poems written for the purposes of propaganda or proselytizing ("sects" and "cults"!), which would place them outside the realm of artistic endeavor and instead in the arena of ideological conversion.

I don't see a difference in degree of influence on the reader's experience between Wright's "A Blessing" and harris's "enough food and a mom." I notice that in referring to Wright's poem, you use the terms "must" and "supposed to" for what the poem asks the reader to feel, as if it were coercion or demand, while of harris's techniques you say they're "proposing and allowing me to

---

20 Robert Frost, "The Figure a Poem Makes," in *The Collected Prose of Robert Frost*, ed. Mark Richardson (Cambridge, MA: The Belknap Press of Harvard University Press, 2007), 132.

21 John Keats, "Ode on a Grecian Urn," in *Essential Keats*, ed. Philip Levine (New York: HarperCollins, 1987), 106.

22 Frost, 132.

imagine a kind of otherwise, to become new through syntax and structure," and that the reader is "swept into" a feeling and "tended to." This seems an unfair distinction to me. The poems employ different craft techniques, but each is a skillfully constructed artifact that tempts the reader to engage with it and, to a degree, surrender to its influence, to feel what the speaker is feeling through the medium of carefully orchestrated language. That, to me, is an essential aspect of all impactful art—seduction. As Susan Sontag has highlighted, there's an eroticism to the act of reading.[23] (Though I don't agree with her desire for an erotics "in place of" a hermeneutics—I believe they must coexist—and I suspect she'd admit that her essay's closing statement was a provocative hyperbole, considering the essay as a whole). A poem asks us to assent to participating with it in a vicarious experience, invites us, seduces us. It does this in any number of formal and structural ways. But it can't *force* us to assent.

Speaking about reading Rilke, William Waters describes his vision of assenting to be a poem's reader—to be its specific addressee: "To read, to be played upon, to give up what we are holding back and to be carried somewhere we did not design to go, is one way we can be transformed in the hands of another. The aesthetic effect of the poem *is* its ethical force, but to know what that means, we must surrender ourselves and become, instead, the poem's reader."[24] This resonates with Rachel Cole's notion of the ethics of mutual satisfaction. In her remarkable close reading of Wallace Stevens's poem "Of Modern Poetry," she concludes that "Stevens anticipates Agamben's suggestion that the purpose of lyric poetry, and the ideal it represents as a model of human encounter, is not [personal] significance but accord: peace. And for Stevens peace is based on a devotion of attention to the reader's pleasure as well as the speaker's, the other's pleasure as well as one's own, and the mutual satisfaction that might result."[25] I also love Annette Gerok-Reiter's perspective on Rilke's imperatives, which I see as relevant to this discussion of the requests a poem makes of its reader. She says that Rilke's imperatives "do not burst out of the poem's space as a direct demand to the reader. Instead [...] they ask the reader to leave his [sic] position as a passive consumer or distanced observer of the poem and to participate in the realization of the poem by helping it to perform itself."[26] These are perspectives on the ways a poem—or any work of art—lures us through the aesthetic effects of its form and invites us to assent to a vicarious experience for a brief time, and in doing so it might

---

[23] See Susan Sontag, "Against Interpretation," in *Against Interpretation and Other Essays* (New York: Farrar, Straus & Giroux, 1966), 3–14.

[24] William Waters, "Rilke's Imperatives." *Poetics Today*, 25.4 (2004), 718.

[25] Rachel Cole, "Rethinking the Value of Lyric Closure: Giorgio Agamben, Wallace Stevens, and the Ethics of Satisfaction." *PMLA*, 126.2 (2011), 396.

[26] Annette Gerok-Reiter. *Wink und Wandlung: Komposition und Poetik in Rilkes "Sonette an Orpheus"* (Tübingen: Niemeyer, 1996), 180.

offer a kind of satisfaction that isn't complacent, but which represents an accord of mind and feeling, one that might spur us to act in the world and so become an *ethical* accord.

As for Machado, she seems to be describing poems that don't impress all the way through: "To compose a ten-line poem, say, with a good first and a devastating last line—it doesn't move me." Well, I don't think that's the type of poem found in this anthology! We've intentionally assembled poems in which, in our view, each element of the poem is essential to the impact of the ending. It seems to me Machado has set up a straw poem. Or perhaps we're not even talking about the same thing she is.

NS: I'm not sure that the goal for me of the poem is peace, that sense of mutual accord. I think I would rather experience uneasiness rather than peace: a dislodging, through image and music and narrative and form, of what I thought I knew. Maybe discord is more ethical for me. But I do like Gerok-Reiter's invitation: that the reader should help the poem perform itself. To that end, in some sense, the life of the form—an architecture which, for me, may have been intended by the author, or may transcend that intent—collaborates with the reader's engagement to create an experience. And certainly in the case of this anthology, as you say—every line is an essential part of an architecture that allows for the impact of the ending.

Though maybe there's a question that remains on the impact of accord versus discord—closing with unity and stability or not. Barbara Hernstein-Smith, in *Poetic Closure*, a tome on endings long perhaps regarded as definitive, has proposed that "[c]losure allows the reader to be satisfied by the failure of continuation or, put another way, it creates in the reader the expectation of nothing."[27] In her definition, the "expectation of nothing" really pivots around "stability, resolution, or equilibrium," or what she calls a sense of "appropriate cessation"—a feeling of finality, completion, and composure for the reader. She compares it to the final mark on Lily Briscoe's canvas in To the Lighthouse, wherein everything else makes sense in light of that final gesture.

I don't think epiphany is inherently unethical, but more and more, I think that perhaps the structure of the epiphany as a closing gesture can pose dangers we should examine closely. That is, this insistence on a feeling of composure and unity (enacted through the form, and to be experienced by the reader) makes me feel uneasy. There certainly isn't composure and unity in the world, or in most lived worlds. I worry that epiphany becomes a kind of synthesizing device, the final mark on the canvas, and you can then walk away and be satiated. To that end, we should look closely at what each epiphany does, why it is placed at the end, and if it asks to be the conclusive "pay-off" of a poem. What are the risks of such a paradigm? I want to return to Aditi Machado again, because I think she engages with these risks so compellingly. For example, when an epiphany

[27] Barbara Hernstein-Smith, *Poetic Closure: A Study of How Poems End* (Chicago: University of Chicago Press, 1968), 34.

caps a poem, even an uncertain one, it might risk becoming an Instagram pull-out quote, the commodity, an invitation by the market to write this way because it gets us more social media shares, what Machado calls the "salable essence of a poem…the money shot."[28]

LH: My understanding of what Cole means about accord and peace is that it can encompass dislocation, provocation, uneasiness, etc. because it's an accord between the poem and the reader, not necessarily an accord between the *subject* of the poem and the reader. A poem might create an accord in terms of a sense of outrage at an injustice, for instance, or an accord in the sense of discovering that someone else has also experienced disorientation or shock or turmoil. My reading of "peace" in the context of Cole's essay is the peace of experiencing human interconnection through the poem, which doesn't necessarily involve a placid aesthetic or formal effect.

I don't accept the characterization of the endings in question—specific poems in the hands of specific critics, but also, as with Hejinian and Machado, epiphanies in general—as too tidy or closed. They're not always closed semantically or chronologically, as you've acknowledged, though clearly you retain greater suspicion of their effects. It seems like a comparison to another artform might be relevant: I wonder if critics of lyrical closure likewise object to, say, harmonic resolution in music. Should songs that resolve harmonically be considered coercive and unethical? Overly simplifying and universalizing? Presenting a false notion of lived experience as neat and tidy? I can't imagine not finding such a claim absurd. There are all sorts of songs, and they don't all resolve harmonically—but the ones that do aren't *wrong* for doing so, nor would it make any sense to me to claim that they're telling an untruth about human experience. Surely there's room for John Cage as well as Mozart, noise music as well as Bebop!

I do admire Machado's discussion of a modern classic, Rilke's "Archaic Torso of Apollo," which for many exemplifies the poetic epiphany. I think her commentary supports my objection to some critics' treatments of epiphany and closure. She recognizes that the final imperative at which the poem shockingly lands is not a closed ending at all: "The end of the poem is there is no end. There is only the rest of time."[29] Nor does the imperative attempt to assert control over the reader or to impart a rigid instruction. As William Waters says, "[I]n these poetic exhortations, the authoritarian dimension of the imperative mood, of which Rilke's editors and critics worry so much, is not in play"[30] and "*How* you must change your life is not specified, since the poem

[28] Machado, 24.

[29] Ibid., 7.

[30] Waters, 723.

is not, and even you yourself are not, in a position to specify what your life is, still less to name the respects in which you do not see it whole. [...] [T]he ethical content of the exhortation is left blank for each recipient to fill in with her own life circumstances and feeling as they are evoked by her own readerly reception of the poem."[31] This reminds me of the effect of Wright's "Lying in a Hammock...," which despite lacking the imperative mood does invite the reader to step into the speaker's subject position as he weighs how he has used his time. (It's clear to me that Wright's poem owes much to Rilke's.)

Another good example of a non-closed epiphany is the end of Keith Flynn's "The Glory Façade," which takes Antoni Gaudí's Basílica de la Sagrada Família as its subject:

> From this I make my life a bell
> and hurl its chime
>   across the expanse,
>   and a gong of years develops,
> buttressed by nothing.
>
> The spool of that life
> is filled with temporary commotions,
>   knowing that a human being
>   in love with mystery
>   is never finished[32]

Here, the ending is memorable and resonant *and* is a type of ongoing "non-ending"—chronologically, propositionally, and even grammatically, given the lack of a period while the rest of the poem is punctuated in a standard fashion. It does offer wisdom, but not a kind that is moralizing or that dictates what the shape of a life ought to look like. As Diane Seuss says, "Poems don't have to resolve. They don't have to save the situation."[33] In Flynn's poem, truth isn't some static certainty, but is "mystery," and when we pursue it, we "are never finished." The poem sends us back into to the world, perhaps inspired, with resounding music in our ears, but in no way having been given a neat and tidy answer to any of life's mysteries.

Regarding Machado's views about the commodification of poetry leading to the urge to write resonant final lines or epiphanies that might serve as "money shots," one counterargument that occurs to me is that what "goes viral" isn't always—probably most often is not—just the ending of

---

[31] Ibid., 717.

[32] Keith Flynn, "The Glory Façade," in *The Skin of Meaning* (Pasadena, CA: Red Hen Press, 2020), 33.

[33] Diane Seuss, "Nothing Is One Thing: An Interview with Diane Seuss." *Lunch Ticket*. https://lunchticket.org/nothing-is-one-thing-an-interview-with-diane-seuss/.

a poem. Lines are pulled from all locations in poems—beginning, middle, and end—or probably just as often an entire poem is shared and it's not just the ending that sparks discussion and sharing.

Furthermore, if Machado wants a poem to endure, as she claims she does, then surely popularity on social media is one way that comes about. It seems hypocritical to idealize work that will endure, but then to claim that when work endures in certain ways it (or its author) is guilty of catering to a capitalist system, especially since "going viral" is almost entirely out of the author's hands and often an author expresses surprise at which poem becomes popular. If they were aiming for Machado's "money shot," there would be no surprise.

Finally, and perhaps most importantly, a poem isn't the same as a commodity, a consumer "product." Poetry has ethical purpose in the ways it helps others feel less alone, enjoy beauty, return with renewed purpose to their lives, and much more. "The aesthetic effect of the poem is its ethical force," as William Waters has said.[34] James Baldwin confided (about fiction, but this applies to literature in general), "You think your pain and your heartbreak are unprecedented in the history of the world, but then you read. It was Dostoevsky and Dickens who taught me that the things that tormented me most were the very things that connected me with all the people who were alive, or who ever had been alive. Only if we face these open wounds in ourselves can we understand them in other people."[35] This, I think, is the kind of "peace" of which Rachel Cole envisions poetry being capable.

NS: I likewise love the (non-)ending of Keith Flynn's poem—it defies grammar and it defies death.

A poem is least likely for me to turn into a commodity when the poem resists a little and pushes back. That is, you can't consume it and own it and use it—as good poems, according to James Longenbach, resist the status of a pragmatic vessel of knowledge, but instead inspire repeated and ongoing readings, growing in meaning and nuance over time.[36] A poem demands that we engage with it again and again, and it is inexhaustible in part because the poem is not exactly the *what* (the subject, the meaning, the *X*) but it is rather the *how* (music, the experience of the song). As Longenbach says, "No one reads Keats's ode 'To Autumn' to be reminded that in September leaves turn colors and fall from the trees; even if we know the poem by heart, we savor the experience of the poem's language as it unfolds in time, luring us forward." [37] We tumble through its ripe sounds as they diminish: "Season of mists and mellow fruitfulness, / Close bosom-friend of the maturing

---

[34] Waters, 718.

[35] Qtd. in Jane Howard, "Doom and Glory of Knowing Who You Are," *Life Magazine*, 54, no. 21 (May 24, 1963), 89. Retrieved from https://books.google.com.

[36] James Longenbach, *Resistance to Poetry* (Chicago: The University of Chicago Press, 2005).

sun." This he describes as lyric knowledge, the pleasurable rediscovery of what we might already know. Though perhaps I'm most interested in a kind of lyric bewilderment and strangeness and doubt alongside this. I keep returning because my cup keeps filling with my unknowing: if poems "must give us back the world somehow," it is a world that is always changing, and we are always changing in it. The form has a life capacious enough for that change. There is ongoing possibility for flux, pleasure, and ricochet between text and world.

We've tried to choose poems for this anthology that do this work: Poems that culminate in "epiphanies," yes—but also many, many other kinds of poems that don't fit into the epiphanic category. Poems that are infinitely repeatable and richer over time. Poems that resist commodification and resist stability. Poems that offer both lyric knowledge and unknowing. Moments of accord and moments of discord. Poems that don't write beyond the surprise.

One thing I think we definitively agree on is this: an excellent ending should not be separable from the fabric of the poem, but rather must emerge organically out of the structure, the build of the poem.

LH: Absolutely. This puts me in mind of a quirky little drawing I made once:

I drew this sketch one evening after meditating on a view from my porch: three power lines intersecting a tree. It struck me as an illustration of the rhetorical and ideational movement of

[37] James Longenbach, *How Poems Get Made* (New York: W.W. Norton, 2018), 12.

some lyric poems. The horizontal lines shouldn't be taken as a representation of the number of lines or stanzas, but of the relative proportions of the poem. Take a poem that's come up in our discussion here—Rilke's "Archaic Torso of Apollo"—as an exemplar. The majority of the poem expounds a central conceit or idea or image; then there's a little lull—a breath—a mental/emotional pause. And then something outlying occurs—a sort of shock—an unexpected, yet organic, outgrowth—a revelation. At first it seems unconnected, but upon consideration can be perceived as part of a larger system hidden beneath the surface.

A Taxonomy of Ending Types

We've come up with a taxonomy of ending types for the poems included in this anthology. It's not exhaustive, of course, and a poem can employ more than one of these strategies, so you'll find several poems cited as examples under multiple categories. We offer very brief commentary on some of the categories; other categories seem sufficiently clear based on the category title, so we've simply listed poems as examples.

We encourage you to devise your own additions to this taxonomy based on poems included here as well as other poems—including your own. Whether you're just starting out as a poet or have been writing for a lifetime, it can be beneficial to examine your poems and consider whether you tend to end them in similar ways. Do you fall back on certain ending types out of instinct, habit, or imitation? Would your work benefit from employing a broader range of ending strategies?

Crescendo/Ecstatic Outburst

This type of epiphanic ending is exemplified by Li-Young Lee's "From Blossoms," where he begins with an image of a bag of roadside peaches, traces their movement from orchard to hands, then segues from embodied to existential pleasure, "O to take what we love inside," bursting at last into the final crescendo: to eat such a peach is actually to live "as if death were nowhere in the background."[38] The body, the mind, exhilarated in this long ("impossible") suspension as we dream death away to live in ripeness: "from joy / to joy to joy, from wing to wing, / from blossom to blossom to / impossible blossom, to sweet impossible blossom."[39]

James Wright's "A Blessing" also falls into this category.

---

[38] Li-Young Lee, "From Blossoms," in *Rose* (Brockport, NY: BOA Editions, 1986): 21.

[39] Ibid.

The Exhortation/Self-Exhortation

More of a cry or demand to the reader or self—the world might be otherwise! An example is Maggie Smith urging, "You could make this place beautiful,"[40] Adam Zagajewski, begging us and himself to "try to praise the mutilated world,"[41] or Ilya Kaminsky exhorting himself, "the darkest / days I must praise."[42]

The Taper-Down

This is a quieter epiphany, with doubt in it. Brigit Pegeen Kelly's "Song," for instance, enacts the passage of time and a kind of haunting that follows the boys because of their cruel and careless action, which at the time they didn't feel the significance of. In C.D. Wright's "Lake Echo, Dear," the speaker narrates the embodied beauty of the world, acknowledges this abundance may or may not change anything.

Enacts its Own Conditions

Ross Gay's "A Small Needful Fact" not only narrates the choke-hold murder of Eric Garner by a police officer, but re-oxygenates Garner's life, in words. Describing how Garner, a horticulturalist, put plants in the earth, the poem plays with the irony that a man who was prevented from breathing made it easier for others to breathe. To trace the poem's form is to see the transformation it enacts: a single sentence of depleting breath as we read is met with the replenishment of breath, by the plants Garner rooted in the earth.

In Kaveh Akbar's "Orchids Are Sprouting from the Floorboards," amidst the speaker's grief, everything in the material world erupts into orchids. We co-inhabit his brutal, stupefying bewilderment in this surreal poem, only finding out at the end the nature of the loss.

In Jorie Graham's "Mother and Child (The Road at the Edge of the Field)," the prolonged and indeterminate winding of syntax creates a wonder-trembling height within the terror and violence of the world. She positions her readers amidst the tendrils of grass, in an ever-modifying sentence, which lasts across 120 lines. The dizzying additions produce near vertigo, awaiting, and bracing for, an uncertain predicate. The final lines, composed of short independent clauses, act as the syntactic and emotive fulcrum, gathering the sensation into a moment of sublime intensity.

---

[40] Maggie Smith, "Good Bones," in *Good Bones* (North Adams, MA: Tupelo Press, 2017): 75.

[41] Adam Zagajewski, "Try to Praise the Mutilated World," in *Without End: New and Selected Poems* (New York: Farrar, Straus and Giroux, 2002): 60.

[42] Ilya Kaminsky, "Author's Prayer," in *Dancing in Odessa* (Dorset, VT: Tupelo Press, 2004): 1.

Paradox and/or Retroactive Alteration of Meaning

In Denis Johnson's "Now," paradox ("nothing" speaking) is revealed through unanticipated grammatical recontextualization that causes the reader to reinterpret what preceded (the meaning of "nothing" changes from "not anything" to a personified nothingness).

Osip Mandelstam's "And I Was Alive" can be read as a contradiction (Claim A and Claim not-A are both asserted) or an enactment of time's ineluctability ("It is now,"[43] but the moment is always passing, so by the time one says "It is now," it is already not that "now").

Repetition/Refrain Takes on Additional Meaning Due to Context &/or Variation of the Repeated Language

In "Duplex," a form that Jericho Brown minted (which guts the sonnet and fuses it with the ghazal and the blues), the refrains change as they cycle through the poem. That is, the poem creates an echo with a difference: the last line is the same as the first in this poem ("A poem is a gesture toward home"[44]), but the final line carries all the violence accrued in the preceding lines.

Novel Syntactic or Formal Structure

In Ruth Stone's "Metamorphosis," the chiasmus "The dancers who cannot sleep, and the sleepers who cannot dance"[45] feels like an ending because it enacts the eternal disjuncture between the past and the present, the dead and the living (sleepers and dancers): X cannot do Y, and Y cannot do X.

Ilya Kaminsky's "Author's Prayer" employs inversion in the final syntax, "the darkest / days I must praise,"[46] to enter the realm of liturgy and the sacred.

In Tiana Clark's "Broken Sestina Reaching for Black Joy," the structure billows and fractures as she struggles to write joy amidst violence.

Ends After Explicitly Resisting an Ending

John Murillo's "Upon Reading That Eric Dolphy Transcribed Even the Calls of Certain Species of Birds" is an example of a long poem that branches between narratives and

---

[43] Osip Mandelstam, "And I Was Alive," trans. Christian Wiman, in *Stolen Air* (New York: Ecco, 2012): 71.

[44] Jericho Brown, "Duplex," in *The Tradition* (Port Townsend, WA: Copper Canyon Press, 2019): 18.

[45] Ruth Stone, "Metamorphosis," in *What Love Comes To: New and Selected Poems* (Port Townsend, WA: Copper Canyon Press, 2008): 143.

[46] Kaminsky, 1.

affects—moving between a suffering sparrow; the speaker's own longing, fear, and limitations; memories of his parents; the transcription of animal noises—bringing the reader to a seeming cusp innumerable times in the poem. But with each almost-ending, Murillo doubles back, holds the reader in thrall, as the bird imagery morphs again.

Ross Gay's "Catalog of Unabashed Gratitude" praises the world in a lush litany of things both beautiful and not-so-beautiful but also not-so-horrible as they might be, all the while apologizing to the reader for the capaciousness of the poet's desire to name and to praise, exhorting the reader to stay with the poem to its eventual end. Somehow these apologies and exhortations make the reader all the more eager to continue on, discovering new imagistic and verbal wonders in line after line after line (*Bellow forth*, *moseying*, *rudbeckia*, *bumblefucked*!).[47]

Comes Full Circle

In B. H. Fairchild's "Beauty," the speaker's present moment causes him to reflect in lush detail on complicated swathes of his past and the notions of masculinity he was raised with. He is transported to a distant time and place, but lands even more solidly in the present moment because of that transport.

Monica Youn's long prose poem "Detail of the Rice Chest" expertly braids considerations of cultural and linguistic artifacts, the speaker's in-between cultural identity, and American prejudices, playing with etymologies and multiple meanings of words throughout, until the speaker unites the disparate filaments in a brilliant final assertion that becomes multivalent due to everything that has been elaborated prior.

Reveals Hidden Subject Matter

This strategy sends the reader back to reconsider everything that led up to the end. The ending speaks what was heretofore unspoken, but was the hidden catalyst for the entire poem. This ricochet backward occurs in Brown's "Duplex" as described above, as the final line repeats but also reconfigures the first line. In Kaveh Akbar's "Orchids Are Sprouting from the Floorboards," the reader trips into a pell-mell dreamscape as orchids erupt into the known world—becoming animal and mineral, memory, and song, and over time becoming the condition of all experience. Only at the very end of the poem, however, do we become privy to the cause, the source of the world's reconfiguration: grief and longing.

---

[47] Ross Gay, "Catalog of Unabashed Gratitude," in *Catalog of Unabashed Gratitude* (Pittsburgh: University of Pittsburgh Press, 2015): 82–93.

Words/Objects Take on Significance Beyond the Norm Due to Context

They're all fine words, sure, but when have *archers*, *blackberry*, or *chink* ever felt so replete with meaning?:

Jack Gilbert, "The Forgotten Dialect of the Heart"

Robert Hass, "Meditation at Lagunitas"

Monica Youn, "Detail of the Rice Chest"

Protean Symbol

In this category, an object shapeshifts or transforms as it recurs, such as Murillo's birds, transforming from a sparrow caught in a car door to a skyful of birds on a day of grieving, to a lover pleading with longing like a sparrow, to the speaker's mother crying like a sparrow, into coupling swans. In the symbol of the bird crystallize, cumulatively, violence, tenderness, and ache. Similarly, Youn crafts a chink in a rice chest where a prince is interred alive, progressively morphing the symbol into an aperture for the gaze of others; into a vulnerability to invasion; into a racist epithet; into the self, closed in the box.

Does Not Fulfill a Structural Expectation or Structure Intentionally Falls Apart

Adam Zagajewski's "Try to Praise the Mutilated World" is built on a refrain, but the refrain doesn't appear at the very end, likely defying the reader's expectation. Instead, the poem ends in image—abiding in the world the refrain has been exhorting us to praise.

Paige Lewis's "You Can Take Off Your Sweater, I've Made Today Warm" takes a visual and rhythmic approach to breaking its established structure of visually even-lined couplets, as the lines rupture apart across the page in the second half of the poem.

Inverts/Subverts a Textual Precedent

Natalie Scenters-Zapico's "Buen Esqueleto" is a retort to and an argument to another poem in this anthology, Maggie Smith's "Good Bones." Unlike Smith's speaker, who withholds the ugliness of the world from her children to protect them, Scenters-Zapico's speaker doesn't try to sell them the world, but rather "show[s] them how to talk / to police without opening the door."[48] Commenting on the textual precedent, she presents a different subject position as well as another ethical and political orientation to the world.

Something Uncanny/Eerie Occurs

Spencer Reece, "ICU"

Louise Glück, "Archaic Fragment"

Realizes an Error, Perceptual Mistake, or Shortcoming

In Ross White's "Quae Nocent Saepe Docent," the speaker wrestles with his own becoming and its source, revising over the course of the poem his notion of who or what might be his teacher. As a ghazal, the sense and content of the word "teacher" pivots, as he re-sees with each couplet.

Likewise, in Yusuf Komunyakaa's "Facing It," the speaker's seeing is amended as he contemplates the names and racialized histories etched in the Vietnam Memorial and his own face seems to disappear into the granite.

In Robert Hayden's "Those Winter Sundays," the speaker describes the harshness of his childhood, when he could not perceive the love of his father, and the narrative distance that allows that love to finally crystallize in the speaker's awareness.

Pulls Together Multiple Thematic Threads of a Long Narrative

In David Kirby's "Get Up, Please," the speaker witnesses a cultural gesture foreign to him during a musical performance, and the later discovery of at least some of what that gesture might mean launches him into a meditation on human relationship and interconnection, mortality, the experience of children in school, Keats's love letters, and the centrality of poetry in the speaker's life, each new facet of the extended meditation seeming seamlessly part of the whole.

Also see:

B. H. Fairchild, "Beauty"

Monica Youn, "Detail of the Rice Chest"

---

[48] Natalie Scenters-Zapico, "Buen Esqueleto," *BuzzFeed News*, July 7, 2017, https://www.buzzfeednews.com/article/nataliescenterszapico/poem-buen-esqueleto-by-natalie-scenters-zapico/.

A Relationship With/Attitude Toward Death Is Arrived At

Christian Wiman, "Love's Last"

Spencer Reece, "ICU"

Lucille Clifton, "1994"

Brigit Pegeen Kelly, "Song"

Sarah Holland-Batt, "The Gift"

Denis Johnson, "Now"

Danusha Laméris, "Edible"

Mystery as a Presence

The ending allows the reader to apprehend the force of mystery, without being able to quite enter it:

Czesław Miłosz, "Encounter"

Or the mystery surrounds us from beginning to end, a sublime force:

Denis Johnson, "Now"

Brigit Pegeen Kelly, "Song"

Or the speaker reaches a place of peace regarding mystery:

Stanley Kunitz, "The Layers"

Reversal of Expectation

The subject or speaker doesn't feel the way we expect them to, or the speaker/poem seems to be making one argument all along, until the final statement, which reveals that the argument is not what we thought it was.

Danusha Laméris, "Edible"

Linda Gregg, "Etiology"

Czesław Miłosz, "Encounter"

Wendy Cope, "To My Husband"

Brigit Pegeen Kelly, "Song"

Jane Hirshfield, "The Supple Deer"

C.D. Wright, "Lake Echo, Dear"

Reframing the Terms of an Unanswerable Question/Dilemma

Linda Pastan, "Ethics"

Ellen Bass, "Relax"

The Trap-Door

This kind of ending, imagined by Connor Yeck with Rebecca Lindenberg,[49] veers away from a concrete sequence of images into sudden abstract thought, like Rilke's "Archaic Torso..."—"you must change your life"[50]—or James Wright's "Lying in a Hammock..." with its final exclamation, "I have wasted my life,"[51] or Thomas James's "Mummy of a Lady Named Jemutesonekh," which closes with the sudden question, "Why do people lie to one another?"[52]

---

[49] "Trap Doors and Lit Fuses: How We End Our Poems," *The Cincinnati Review*, October 27, 2022, https://www.cincinnatireview.com/on-craft/trapdoors-lit-fuses-how-we-end-our-poems/.

[50] Rainer Maria Rilke, "Archaic Torso of Apollo," trans. Stephen Mitchell. https://poets.org/poem/archaic-torso-apollo/.

[51] Wright, "Lying in a Hammock...," 114.

[52] Thomas James, "Mummy of a Lady Named Jemutesonekh," in *Letters to a Stranger* (Saint Paul, MN: Graywolf Press, 2008), 80.

Bibliography

Auden, W. H. *W. H. Auden: Collected Poems*, ed. Edward Mendelson. New York: Vintage, 2007.

Baxter, Charles. "Against Epiphanies." In *Burning Down the House*, 51–77. Saint Paul, MN: Graywolf Press, 1997.

Boruch, Marianne. "The End Inside It," *New England Review* 33.2 (2012). Retrieved July 8, 2024. https://www.nereview.com/back-issues/vol-33-1-4-2012-2013/vol-33-2-2012/.

Brown, Jericho. "Duplex." In *The Tradition*, 18. Port Townsend, WA: Copper Canyon Press, 2019.

Cole, Rachel. "Rethinking the Value of Lyric Closure: Giorgio Agamben, Wallace Stevens, and the Ethics of Satisfaction." *PMLA* (126.2, 2011): 383–97.

Edmond, Jacob. "The Closures of the Open Text: Lyn Hejinian's 'Paradise Found.'" *Contemporary Literature* (50.2, 2009): 240–72.

Flynn, Keith. "The Glory Façade." In *The Skin of Meaning*, 32–3. Pasadena, CA: Red Hen Press, 2020.

Frost, Robert. "The Figure a Poem Makes." In *The Collected Prose of Robert Frost*, ed. Mark Richardson, 131–3. Cambridge, MA: The Belknap Press of Harvard University Press, 2007.

Gay, Ross. "Catalog of Unabashed Gratitude." In *Catalog of Unabashed Gratitude*, 82–93. Pittsburgh: University of Pittsburgh Press, 2015.

Gerok-Reiter, Annette. *Wink und Wandlung: Komposition und Poetik in Rilkes "Sonette an Orpheus."* Tübingen: Niemeyer, 1996.

harris, francine j. "enough food and a mom," in *Play Dead*, 83. New Gloucester, ME: Alice James Books, 2016.

Hejinian, Lyn. "The Rejection of Closure." In *The Language of Inquiry*, 1st ed., 40–58. Berkeley: University of California Press, 2000.

Hernstein-Smith, Barbara. *Poetic Closure: A Study of How Poems End.* Chicago: University of Chicago Press, 1968.

Howard, Jane. "Doom and Glory of Knowing Who You Are." *Life Magazine*, 54, no. 21 (May 24, 1963): 89. https://books.google.com/.

James, Thomas. "Mummy of a Lady Named Jemutesonekh." In *Letters to a Stranger*, 79–80. Saint Paul, MN: Graywolf Press, 2008.

Kaminsky, Ilya. "Author's Prayer." In *Dancing in Odessa*, 1. Dorset, VT: Tupelo Press, 2004.

Keats, John. "Ode on a Grecian Urn." In *Essential Keats*, ed. Philip Levine, 104–6. New York: HarperCollins, 1987.

Lee, Li-Young. "From Blossoms." In *Rose*, 21. Brockport, NY: BOA Editions, 1986.
Longenbach, James. *How Poems Get Made*. New York: W.W. Norton, 2018.
——. *The Resistance to Poetry*. Chicago: The University of Chicago Press, 2005.
Machado, Aditi. *The End*. New York: Ugly Duckling Presse, 2020.
Mandelstam, Osip. "And I Was Alive." Translated by Christian Wiman. In *Stolen Air*, 71. New York: Ecco, 2012.
Phillips, Carl. The Harwood-Cole Literary Lecture, Warren Wilson College, Swannanoa, NC. Feb. 25, 2024.
Raab, Lawrence. "Uncertain Clarity: Some Ways Poems End," *Mentor and Muse: Essays From Poets to Poets*. Retrieved July 8, 2024. https://mentorandmuse.net/lawrence-raab/.
Seuss, Diane. "Nothing Is One Thing: An Interview with Diane Seuss." *Lunch Ticket*. https://lunchticket.org/nothing-is-one-thing-an-interview-with-diane-seuss/.
Smith, Maggie. "Good Bones." In *Good Bones*, 75. North Adams, MA: Tupelo Press, 2017.
Scenters-Zapico, Natalie. "Buen Esqueleto." *BuzzFeed News*, July 7, 2017. Retrieved July 8, 2024. https://www.buzzfeednews.com/article/nataliescenterszapico/poem-buen-esqueleto-by-natalie-scenters-zapico/.
Sontag, Susan. "Against Interpretation". In *Against Interpretation and Other Essays*, 3–14. New York: Farrar, Straus & Giroux, 1966.
Ștefănescu, Alina. "Interview with Alina Ștefănescu." *Mentor & Muse*. Retrieved May 28, 2024. https://mentorandmuse.net/alina-stefanescu/.
Stone, Ruth. "Metamorphosis." In *What Love Comes To: New and Selected Poems*, 143. Port Townsend, WA: Copper Canyon Press, 2008.
Waters, William. "Rilke's Imperatives." *Poetics Today* (25.4, 2004): 711–30.
Wright, James. "A Blessing." In *Collected Poems*, 135. Middletown, CT: Wesleyan University Press, 1971.
——. "Lying in a Hammock at William Duffy's Farm in Pine Island, Minnesota." Ibid., 114.
Zagajewski, Adam. "Try to Praise the Mutilated World." In *Without End: New and Selected Poems*, 60. New York: Farrar, Straus and Giroux, 2002.

Breaking *into* Blossom

Danusha Laméris

Edible

We want it all: Potatoes pulled up
from under their poison foliage,
the artichoke's heart, scraped clean,
the tender bodies of crustaceans, broken
from their calcified shells, saffron stamens,
plucked from the crocus's center. Bark
of cinnamon trees, slow sugar tapped
from the maple. The golden vomit of bees,
pried from its waxen vaults. Even,
for some, the delicate crunch of crickets,
or hind legs of lamb, still tinged with blood.
The world is such an unexpected feast.
I think of my friend, Christopher,
who, when he found himself dying,
early one spring, kept telling us
how *this* was the best part—
the letting go. As if, in his hunger,
he'd somehow broken into death's core,
torn off the husk, the brittle shell,
found, inside, the succulent heart,
and savored it.

James Wright

A Blessing

Just off the highway to Rochester, Minnesota,
Twilight bounds softly forth on the grass.
And the eyes of those two Indian ponies
Darken with kindness.
They have come gladly out of the willows
To welcome my friend and me.
We step over the barbed wire into the pasture
Where they have been grazing all day, alone.
They ripple tensely, they can hardly contain their happiness
That we have come.
They bow shyly as wet swans. They love each other.
There is no loneliness like theirs.
At home once more,
They begin munching the young tufts of spring in the darkness.
I would like to hold the slenderer one in my arms,
For she has walked over to me
And nuzzled my left hand.
She is black and white,
Her mane falls wild on her forehead,
And the light breeze moves me to caress her long ear
That is delicate as the skin over a girl's wrist.
Suddenly I realize
That if I stepped out of my body I would break
Into blossom.

Ilya Kaminsky

Author's Prayer

If I speak for the dead, I must leave
this animal of my body,

I must write the same poem over and over,
for an empty page is the white flag of their surrender.

If I speak for them, I must walk on the edge
of myself, I must live as a blind man

who runs through rooms without
touching the furniture.

Yes, I live. I can cross the streets asking "What year is it?"
I can dance in my sleep and laugh

in front of the mirror.
Even sleep is a prayer, Lord,

I will praise your madness, and
in a language not mine, speak

of music that wakes us, music
in which we move. For whatever I say

is a kind of petition, and the darkest
days must I praise.

Richard Siken

Scheherazade

Tell me about the dream where we pull the bodies out of the lake
and dress them in warm clothes again.
How it was late, and no one could sleep, the horses running
until they forget that they are horses.
It's not like a tree where the roots have to end somewhere,
it's more like a song on a policeman's radio,
how we rolled up the carpet so we could dance, and the days
were bright red, and every time we kissed there was another apple
to slice into pieces.
Look at the light through the windowpane. That means it's noon, that means
we're inconsolable.
Tell me how all this, and love too, will ruin us.
These, our bodies, possessed by light.
Tell me we'll never get used to it.

C. D. Wright

Lake Echo, Dear

Is the woman in the pool of light
really reading or just staring
at what is written

Is the man walking in the soft rain
naked or is it the rain
that makes his shirt transparent

The boy in the iron cot
is he asleep or still
fingering the springs underneath

Did you honestly believe
three lives could be complete

The bottle of green liquid
on the sill is it real

The bottle on the peeling sill
is it filled with green

Or is the liquid an illusion
of fullness

How summer's children turn
into fish and rain softens men

How the elements of summer
nights bid us to get down with each other
on the unplaned floor

And this feels painfully beautiful
whether or not
it will change the world one drop

Marie Howe

Part of Eve's Discussion

It was like the moment when a bird decides not to eat from your hand,
and flies, just before it flies, the moment the rivers seem to still
and stop because a storm is coming, but there is no storm, as when
a hundred starlings lift and bank together before they wheel and drop,
very much like the moment, driving on bad ice, when it occurs to you
your car could spin, just before it slowly begins to spin, like
the moment just before you forgot what it was you were about to say,
it was like that, and after that, it was still like that, only
all the time.

Cameron Awkward-Rich

Meditations in an Emergency

I wake up & it breaks my heart. I draw the blinds & the thrill of rain breaks my heart. I go outside. I ride the train, walk among the buildings, men in Monday suits. The flight of doves, the city of tents beneath the underpass, the huddled mass, old women hawking roses, & children all of them, break my heart. There's a dream I have in which I love the world. I run from end to end like fingers through her hair. There are no borders, only wind. Like you, I was born. Like you, I was raised in the institution of dreaming. Hand on my heart. Hand on my stupid heart.

Ross Gay

A Small Needful Fact

Is that Eric Garner worked
for some time for the Parks and Rec.
Horticultural Department, which means,
perhaps, that with his very large hands,
perhaps, in all likelihood,
he put gently into the earth
some plants which, most likely,
some of them, in all likelihood,
continue to grow, continue
to do what such plants do, like house
and feed small and necessary creatures,
like being pleasant to touch and smell,
like converting sunlight
into food, like making it easier
for us to breathe.

Philip Metres

Black Site (Exhibit I)

Whenever I saw

a fly in my cell

I was filled

with joy

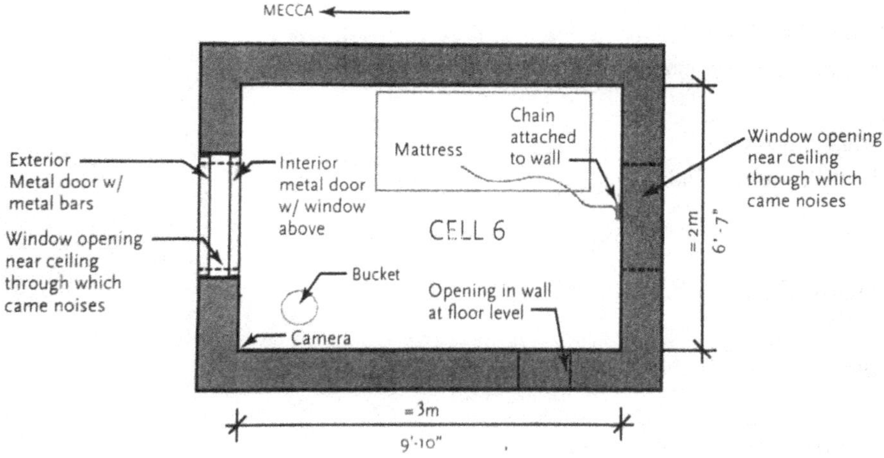

though I wished for it

to slip under the door

so it would not be

imprisoned itself

Louise Glück

Archaic Fragment

I was trying to love matter.
I taped a sign over the mirror:
You cannot hate matter and love form.

It was a beautiful day, though cold.
This was, for me, an extravagantly emotional gesture.

.......your poem:
tried, but could not.

I taped a sign over the first sign:
Cry, weep, thrash yourself, rend your garments—

List of things to love:
dirt, food, shells, human hair.

.......said
tasteless excess. Then I

rent the signs.

AIAIAIAI cried
the naked mirror.

Jean Valentine

Door in the Mountain

Never ran this hard through the valley
never ate so many stars

I was carrying a dead deer
tied on to my neck and shoulders

deer legs hanging in front of me
heavy on my chest

People are not wanting
to let me in

Door in the mountain
let me in

John Murillo

Upon Reading That Eric Dolphy Transcribed Even the Calls of Certain Species of Birds

I think first of two sparrows I met when walking home,
late night years ago, in another city, not unlike this—the one

bird frantic, attacking I thought, the way she swooped
down, circled my head, and flailed her wings in my face;

how she seemed to scream each time I swung; how she
dashed back and forth between me and a blood-red Corolla

parked near the opposite curb; how, finally, I understood:
I spied another bird, also calling, its foot inexplicably

caught in the car's closed door, beating its whole bird
body against it. Trying, it appeared, to bang himself free.

And who knows how long he'd been there, wailing. Who
knows—he and the other I mistook, at first, for a bat.

They called to me—something between squawk and chirp,
something between song and prayer—to do something,

anything. And, like any good god, I disappeared. Not
indifferent, exactly. But with things to do. And, most likely,

on my way home from another heartbreak. Call it 1997,
and say I'm several thousand miles from home. By which

I mean those were the days I made of everyone a love song.
By which I mean I was lonely and unrequited. But that's

not quite it either. Truth is, I did manage to find a few
to love me, but couldn't always love them back. The Rasta

law professor. The firefighter's wife. The burlesque dancer
whose daughter blackened drawings with *m*s to mean

the sky was full of birds the day her daddy died. I think
his widow said he drowned one morning on a fishing trip.

Anyway, I'm digressing. But if you asked that night—
did I mention it was night?—why I didn't even try

to jimmy the lock to spring the sparrow, I couldn't say,
truthfully, that it had anything to do with envy, with wanting

a woman to plead as deeply for me as these sparrows did,
one for the other. No. I'd have said something, instead,

about the neighborhood itself, the car thief shot a block
and a half east the week before. Or about the men

I came across nights prior, sweat-slicked and shirtless,
grappling in the middle of the street, the larger one's chest

pressed to the back of the smaller, bruised and bleeding
both. I know you thought this was about birds,

but stay with me. I left them both in the street—
the same street where I'd leave the sparrows—the men

embracing and, for all one knows (especially one not
from around there), they could have been lovers—

the one whispering an old, old tune into the ear
of the other—*Baby, baby, don't leave me this way*. I left

the men where I'd leave the sparrows and their song.
And as I walked away, I heard one of the men call to me,

please or *help* or *brother* or some such. And I didn't break
stride, not one bit. It's how I've learned to save myself.

Let me try this another way. Call it 1977. And say
I'm back west, South Central Los Angeles. My mother

and father at it again. But this time in the street,
broad daylight, and all the neighbors watching. One,

I think his name was Sonny, runs out from his duplex
to pull my father off. You see where I'm going with this?

My mother crying out, fragile as a sparrow. Sonny
fighting my father, fragile as a sparrow. And me,

years later, trying to get it all down. As much for you—
I'm saying—as for me. Sonny catches a left, lies flat

on his back, blood starting to pool and his own
wife wailing. My mother wailing, and traffic backed,

now, half a block. Horns, whistles, and soon sirens.
1977. Summer. And all the trees full of birds. Hundreds,

I swear. And since I'm the one writing it, I'll tell you
they were crying. Which brings me back to Dolphy

and his transcribing. The jazzman, I think, wanted only
to get it down pure. To get it down exact—the animal

racking itself against a car's steel door, the animals
in the trees reporting, the animals we make of ourselves

and one another. Stay with me now. Don't leave me.
Days after the dustup, my parents took me to the park.

And in this park was a pond, and in this pond were birds.
Not sparrows, but swans. And my father spread a blanket

and brought from a basket some apples and a paring knife.
Summertime. My mother wore sunglasses. And long sleeves.

My father, now sober, cursed himself for leaving the radio.
But my mother forgave him, and said, as she caressed

the back of his hand, that we could just listen to the swans.
And we listened. And I watched. Two birds coupling,

one beating its wings as it mounted the other. Summer,
1977. I listened. And watched. When my parents made love

late into that night, I covered my ears in the next room,
scanning the encyclopedia for swans. It meant nothing to me—

then, at least—but did you know the collective noun
for swans is a *lamentation*? And is a lamentation not

its own species of song? What a woman wails, punch drunk
in the street? Or what a widow might sing, learning her man

was drowned by swans? A lamentation of them? Imagine
the capsized boat, the panicked man, struck about the eyes,

nose, and mouth each time he comes up for air. Imagine
the birds coasting away and the waters suddenly calm.

Either trumpet swans or mutes. The dead man's wife
running for help, crying to any who'd listen. A lamentation.

And a city busy saving itself. I'm digressing, sure. But
did you know that to digress means to stray from the flock?

When I left my parents' house, I never looked back. By which
I mean I made like a god and disappeared. As when I left

the sparrows. And the copulating swans. As when someday
I'll leave this city. Its every flailing, its every animal song.

William Matthews

Mingus in Diaspora

You could say, I suppose, that he ate his way out,
like the prisoner who starts a tunnel with a spoon,
or you could say he was one in whom nothing was lost,
who took it all in, or that he was big as a bus.

He would say, and he did, in one of those blurred
melismatic slaloms his sentences ran—for all
the music was in his speech: swift switches of tempo,
stop-time, double time (he could *talk* in 6/8),

"I just ruined my body." And there, Exhibit A,
it stood, that Parthenon of fat, the tenant voice
lifted, as we say, since words are a weight, and music.
Silence is lighter than air, for the air we know

rises but to the edge of the atmosphere.
You have to pick up The Bass, as Mingus called
his, with audible capitals, and think of the slow years
the wood spent as a tree, which might well have been

enough for wood, and think of the skill the bassmaker
carried without great thought of it from home
to the shop and back for decades, and know
what bassists before you have played, and know

how much of this is stored in The Bass like energy
in a spring and know how much you must coax out.
How easy it would be, instead, to pull a sword
from a stone. But what's inside the bass wants out,

the way one day you will. Religious stories are rich
in symmetry. You must release as much of this hoard
as you can, little by little, in perfect time,
as the work of the body becomes a body of work.

Jack Gilbert

The Forgotten Dialect of the Heart

How astonishing it is that language can almost mean,
and frightening that it does not quite. *Love*, we say,
God, we say, *Rome* and *Michiko*, we write, and the words
get it all wrong. We say bread and it means according
to which nation. French has no word for home,
and we have no word for strict pleasure. A people
in northern India is dying out because their ancient
tongue has no words for endearment. I dream of lost
vocabularies that might express some of what
we no longer can. Maybe the Etruscan texts would
finally explain why the couples on their tombs
are smiling. And maybe not. When the thousands
of mysterious Sumerian tablets were translated,
they seemed to be business records. But what if they
are poems or psalms? My joy is the same as twelve
Ethiopian goats standing silent in the morning light.
O Lord, thou art slabs of salt and ingots of copper,
as grand as ripe barley lithe under the wind's labor.
Her breasts are six white oxen loaded with bolts
of long-fibered Egyptian cotton. My love is a hundred
pitchers of honey. Shiploads of thuya are what
my body wants to say to your body. Giraffes are this
desire in the dark. Perhaps the spiral Minoan script
is not language but a map. What we feel most has
no name but amber, archers, cinnamon, horses, and birds.

Czesław Miłosz

Encounter

We were riding through frozen fields in a wagon at dawn.
A red wing rose in the darkness.

And suddenly a hare ran across the road.
One of us pointed to it with his hand.

That was long ago. Today neither of them is alive,
Not the hare, nor the man who made the gesture.

O my love, where are they, where are they going
The flash of a hand, streak of movement, rustle of pebbles.
I ask not out of sorrow, but in wonder.

Wilno, 1936

Jane Hirshfield

The Supple Deer

The quiet opening
between fence strands
perhaps eighteen inches.

Antlers to hind hooves,
four feet off the ground,
the deer poured through.

No tuft of the coarse white belly hair left behind.

I don't know how a stag turns
into a stream, an arc of water.
I have never felt such accurate envy.

Not of the deer:

To be that porous, to have such largeness pass through me.

W. S. Merwin

Vixen

Comet of stillness princess of what is over
        high note held without trembling without voice without sound
aura of complete darkness keeper of the kept secrets
        of the destroyed stories the escaped dreams the sentences
never caught in words warden of where the river went
        touch of its surface sibyl of the extinguished
window onto the hidden place and the other time
        at the foot of the wall by the road patient without waiting
in the full moonlight of autumn at the hour when I was born
        you no longer go out like a flame at the sight of me
you are still warmer than the moonlight gleaming on you
        even now you are unharmed even now perfect
as you have always been now when your light paws are running
        on the breathless night on the bridge with one end I remember you
when I have heard you the soles of my feet have made answer
        when I have seen you I have waked and slipped from the calendars
from the creeds of difference and the contradictions
        that were my life and all the crumbling fabrications
as long as it lasted until something that we were
        had ended when you are no longer anything
let me catch sight of you again going over the wall
        and before the garden is extinct and the woods are figures
guttering on a screen let my words find their own
        places in the silence after the animals

Matthew Olzmann

Nate Brown Is Looking for a Moose

Shrouded in fog, dignified and reticent: a moose.
When Ross White goes outside in Vermont,
he sees one immediately.

When Jamaal May goes outside, he sees one as well.
As if they are everywhere.

But when Nate Brown goes outside, he sees
only the absence of a moose, spaces
where one might have stood but no longer stands.

He's been hoping to see one for years.
So he practices his moose call, and nothing happens.
He stands tiptoe, on one leg,
narrows his eyes. Nothing happens.

What he has now is a mission, a quest,
a calling that can't be denied.

It's dusk and he stares into the dark. The world
is full of dogwoods and elm trees, and behind the branches,
ten thousand more—all leafy and stupid
and yielding no answers.

What do I mean? I mean
despite everything, we might search
for something and never find it.

When I was a teenager, several of my friends
suddenly found God.
I tried, but found only pocket lint and angst.

The loser of some holy scavenger hunt,
the last to cross the finish line,

kneeling in church, whispering
to heaven: *Dude, where are you?*

What made it worse was everyone's conviction.
The candles and prayer groups,
the smugness of their repeating, *Well, you know,*
if you look behind you and see only one set of footprints—

What makes Nate Brown's quest equally difficult
is how our friend Chip Cheek leans back in his chair
and says, *Oh Man—out here they grow big as dinosaurs.*

And how Kellam Ayers's eyes fill with mist
when she nods and says, *Yes, they're almost   magical.*

And so a man goes back into the fields
and tries not to move. Goes
out to the forest and tries not to move. Goes
down to the river
and pretends he's part of that river.

He is a stone, a branch, a fallen maple leaf.
He is (sort of) patient
and he'll see this thing or hold his breath forever.

I think of myself as a teenager and how
I'm no different now.

At home, my wife has a numbness, a weakness that spreads
through her body and no doctors
can figure it out. When she sleeps,

I'm afraid of everything and I pray into her hair
like I'm young again
on my knees in a church, in search of an answer.

Sometimes I go outside, and the dark is so prodigious—
the way it remedies everything by covering everything.

I like thinking of how my friend stares
down this same darkness
as if it will offer the index to some temporal secret.

What we're looking for are miracles.

Out there—
there could be nothing.

Or there could be antlers and hooves.
Lumbering mysteries.
They plod across the quiet fields.

Jordan Rice

Lost Body

Today they are talking on the radio about
how to remember your infant, and not leave them

in car seats for swelter to unspeak them

or in the cold
various parents raise their shoulders against here

in the grocery store parking lot while I am coming out
to my mother, over the phone, temperate zones away, saying

how I must change, that I cannot stand this body any longer,

the one she remembered
held and fed and would not hold only once—when I fell

beneath the rear tractor wheel, rolled under before anyone
could stop the bush hog. This is the story she is telling me now—

again as though I haven't heard,
or can't remember what happened, like the first year after,

which is blank but for scars, and the sudden noise of an engine
causing night terrors—that she stood over me in that field
only thinking: my son my son.

Yehoshua November

Conjoined Twins

My father was a resident in the hospital
when my young mother gave birth to them. Two bodies
and one heart.

And hearing that the pathologists at that teaching institution
were coming to learn the lessons
science's rare cases could teach,
my father turned the combination
on his locker and concealed the stillborn baby boys in a box.

Early the next morning, another Jewish resident
stood over the bodies with my father,
performed the ritual circumcisions in the silence
of an unoccupied delivery room.
"Choose names you would not otherwise use,"
the rabbi had instructed over the phone.

At the burial my father asked why
this had happened. "Perhaps you are not
as religious as you should be," the rabbi answered.
And the answer plunged God
into concealment for my father.

"I looked quickly
and saw them embracing,"
my mother later said
of the two boys, who were to be born
between Purim and Passover.

One was named Mordechai,
who gathered all the Jews
when they thought they had been forsaken.
And one was named Pesach,
the holiday when all Jews,

even idol worshippers,
were freed,
as long as they desired to go.

And they left their bondage
and arrived at the mountain
where, the Midrash states,
they camped in the desert
like one man
with one heart.

Brigit Pegeen Kelly

Song

Listen: there was a goat's head hanging by ropes in a tree.
All night it hung there and sang. And those who heard it
Felt a hurt in their hearts and thought they were hearing
The song of a night bird. They sat up in their beds, and then
They lay back down again. In the night wind, the goat's head
Swayed back and forth, and from far off it shone faintly
The way the moonlight shone on the train track miles away
Beside which the goat's headless body lay. Some boys
Had hacked its head off. It was harder work than they had imagined.
The goat cried like a man and struggled hard. But they
Finished the job. They hung the bleeding head by the school
And then ran off into the darkness that seems to hide everything.
The head hung in the tree. The body lay by the tracks.
The head called to the body. The body to the head.
They missed each other. The missing grew large between them,
Until it pulled the heart right out of the body, until
The drawn heart flew toward the head, flew as a bird flies
Back to its cage and the familiar perch from which it trills.
Then the heart sang in the head, softly at first and then louder,
Sang long and low until the morning light came up over
The school and over the tree, and then the singing stopped....
The goat had belonged to a small girl. She named
The goat Broken Thorn Sweet Blackberry, named it after
The night's bush of stars, because the goat's silky hair
Was dark as well water, because it had eyes like wild fruit.
The girl lived near a high railroad track. At night
She heard the trains passing, the sweet sound of the train's horn
Pouring softly over her bed, and each morning she woke
To give the bleating goat his pail of warm milk. She sang
Him songs about girls with ropes and cooks in boats.
She brushed him with a stiff brush. She dreamed daily
That he grew bigger, and he did. She thought her dreaming
Made it so. But one night the girl didn't hear the train's horn,
And the next morning she woke to an empty yard. The goat

Was gone. Everything looked strange. It was as if a storm
Had passed through while she slept, wind and stones, rain
Stripping the branches of fruit. She knew that someone
Had stolen the goat and that he had come to harm. She called
To him. All morning and into the afternoon, she called
And called. She walked and walked. In her chest a bad feeling
Like the feeling of the stones gouging the soft undersides
Of her bare feet. Then somebody found the goat's body
By the high tracks, the flies already filling their soft bottles
At the goat's torn neck. Then somebody found the head
Hanging in a tree by the school. They hurried to take
These things away so that the girl would not see them.
They hurried to raise money to buy the girl another goat.
They hurried to find the boys who had done this, to hear
Them say it was a joke, a joke, it was nothing but a joke....
But listen: here is the point. The boys thought to have
Their fun and be done with it. It was harder work than they
Had imagined, this silly sacrifice, but they finished the job,
Whistling as they washed their large hands in the dark.
What they didn't know was that the goat's head was already
Singing behind them in the tree. What they didn't know
Was that the goat's head would go on singing, just for them,
Long after the ropes were down, and that they would learn to listen,
Pail after pail, stroke after patient stroke. They would
Wake in the night thinking they heard the wind in the trees
Or a night bird, but their hearts beating harder. There
Would be a whistle, a hum, a high murmur, and, at last, a song,
The low song a lost boy sings remembering his mother's call.
Not a cruel song, no, no, not cruel at all. This song
Is sweet. It is sweet. The heart dies of this sweetness.

Linda Pastan

Ethics

In ethics class so many years ago
our teacher asked this question every fall:
if there were a fire in a museum
which would you save, a Rembrandt painting
or an old woman who hadn't many
years left anyhow? Restless on hard chairs
caring little for pictures or old age
we'd opt one year for life, the next for art
and always half-heartedly. Sometimes
the woman borrowed my grandmother's face
leaving her usual kitchen to wander
some drafty, half-imagined museum.
One year, feeling clever, I replied
why not let the woman decide herself?
Linda, the teacher would report, eschews
the burdens of responsibility.
This fall in a real museum I stand
before a real Rembrandt, old woman,
or nearly so, myself. The colors
within this frame are darker than autumn,
darker even than winter—the browns of earth,
though earth's most radiant elements burn
through the canvas. I know now that woman
and painting and season are almost one
and all beyond saving by children.

James Dickey

The Strength of Fields

...a separation from the world,
a penetration to some source of power
and a life-enhancing return...
—Van Gennep, *Rites de Passage*

Moth-force a small town always has,

Given the night.

What field-forms can be,
Outlying the small civic light-decisions over
A man walking near home?
Men are not where he is
Exactly now, but they are around him around him like the strength

Of fields. The solar system floats on
Above him in town-moths.
Tell me, train-sound,
With all your long-lost grief,
what I can give.
Dear Lord of all the fields
what am I going to *do*?
Street-lights, blue-force and frail
As the homes of men, tell me how to do it how
To withdraw how to penetrate and find the source
Of the power you always had
light as a moth, and rising
With the level and moonlit expansion
Of the fields around, and the sleep of hoping men.

You? I? What difference is there? We can all be saved

By a secret blooming. Now as I walk
The night   and you walk with me.   we know simplicity
Is close to the source that sleeping men
Search for in their home-deep beds.

We know that the sun is away   we know that the sun can be conquered   By moths, in blue home-town air.
The stars splinter, pointed and wild. The dead lie under
The pastures.   They look on and help.   Tell me, freight-train,
When there is no one else
To hear.   Tell me in a voice the sea
Would have, if it had not a better one: as it lifts,
Hundreds of miles away, its fumbling, deep-structured roar
Like the profound, unstoppable craving
Of nations for their wish.
Hunger, time and the moon:

The moon lying on the brain
as on the excited sea   as on
The strength of fields.   Lord, let me shake
With purpose.   Wild hope can always spring
From tended strength.   Everything is in that.
That and nothing but kindness.   More kindness, dear Lord
Of the renewing green.   That is where it all has to start:
With the simplest things.   More kindness will do nothing less
Than save every sleeping one
And night-walking one

Of us.
My life belongs to the world. I will do what I can.

Ellen Bass

Relax

Bad things are going to happen.
Your tomatoes will grow a fungus
and your cat will get run over.
Someone will leave the bag with the ice cream
melting in the car and throw
your blue cashmere sweater in the dryer.
Your husband will sleep
with a girl your daughter's age, her breasts spilling
out of her blouse. Or your wife
will remember she's a lesbian
and leave you for the woman next door. The other cat—
the one you never really liked—will contract a disease
that requires you to pry open its feverish mouth
every four hours. Your parents will die.
No matter how many vitamins you take,
how much Pilates, you'll lose your keys,
your hair, and your memory. If your daughter
doesn't plug her heart
into every live socket she passes,
you'll come home to find your son has emptied
the refrigerator, dragged it to the curb,
and called the used-appliance store for a pick up—drug money.
The Buddha tells a story of a woman chased by a tiger.
When she comes to a cliff, she sees a sturdy vine
and climbs half way down. But there's also a tiger below.
And two mice—one white, one black—scurry out
and begin to gnaw at the vine. At this point
she notices a wild strawberry growing from a crevice.
She looks up, down, at the mice.
Then she eats the strawberry.
So here's the view, the breeze, the pulse
in your throat. Your wallet will be stolen, you'll get fat,
slip on the bathroom tiles of a foreign hotel

and crack your hip. You'll be lonely.
Oh, taste how sweet and tart
the red juice is, how the tiny seeds
crunch between your teeth.

Jay Hopler

love & the memory of it

spook not at the shook world w/ all its viruses & murder hornets
instead that summer evening call to mind when you drove alone over iowa
the light in the fields how long it was how in love you were w/ it
& the air & the world & that girl that atomic girl you would one day marry
or summon up a summer evening half a life from then & the park by the river the way her laughter
echoed off the rocks
in sparks that sighed
into the water

it was she that lit the world just then
& not that ember of a sun
her light like a struck string fretting its zing against the pic-nic tables

may that be the music you hear
when they unplug the ventilator

Tiana Clark

Broken Sestina Reaching for Black Joy

Yesterday I was smashed with the rush of fresh honeysuckle
from the greenway near my house where I walk every day.
I've been trying to write a poem about buried Black bodies
but all I want to write about is Black joy and my pleasure
and Black love and Black lives that don't end with viral death,
so I've stopped consuming the news. I've logged off of social

media for a break. Black bodies are buried in the stickiness of history
every day bodies become the next viral death. And yet, each day
I want to write a poem about pleasure. Black pleasure at the root
instead of viral death. What name now? What Black litany? What
Black elegy is repeated on the news? This cycle: Daunte Wright.
I don't know the details yet, because I can't handle the details yet,
but I am mourning him still. This stanza broke the rules. So, what?

This stanza will break back inside the form of honeycomb to suck
the lyric into compression, reboot restraint, the grief-joy every day
when I walk around Sylvan Park near a broken track of burned Black bodies
but all I want to write about is Black joy and *pleasure pleasure pleasure*
please ... and Black love and Black lives that don't end with viral death,
so I've stopped consuming the news. I've deleted all my social-media

apps, but logged back in later, saw your name repeating as death
media. Fresh honeysuckle at dusk smells like sweet earth, ripe bodies,
warm floral notes. Heady with romance and nectar. It permeates the day
I walk over the bridge where I often see a single blue heron, not social,
standing stone-still stalking Richland Creek fringed with honeysuckle,
which reminds me of any Mary Oliver poem, such pastoral pleasures.

(I'm also still thinking about Claudia Rankine's blossoming blood
list of Black bodies broken from police brutality inside *Citizen*
on page 134. The memoriam fades into the sheer forecast of names
we know will come.) I picked the sestina for its obsessive listing
and twisting. I selected the sestina to probe a problem I can name

but can't answer. The end words are planets orbiting the math.

Pleasure.
Death.
Honeysuckle
Black bodies.
Social / Media.
Every day.

Every day here are some of the plants and trees I've collected during my walks. I take pictures on my phone so an app can tell me what they are: ginkgo, bristly locust, maiden pink, garden star-of-Bethlehem, wild pansy, birdeye speedwell, eastern redbud, Japanese cherry, apricot, peach, American holly, beefsteak plant, maypop, common blue wood aster. calico aster, eastern white pine, southern sugar maple, scarlet morning glory.

Every day I walk past Dutchman's Curve, the eerie site of the Great Train Wreck of 1918. Deadliest train wreck in American history which killed 101 people, mostly African Americans, headed to a factory to make weapons for World War I. They were stuffed in rickety wooden cars in the front due to segregation. The front being the most dangerous spot on a train about to crash, while white bodies were in steel Pullman cars in the back, protected.

But at 100 mph the wooden cars with Black bodies telescoped, splintered, and caught fire immediately upon impact with another train on the blind curve. The historian David Ewing describes bodies writhing in pain. Bodies without heads and limbs. Bodies unidentified, maimed: "The African-Americans that were on this train did not have a chance to survive, given where they were."

> "The cornfield on both sides of the track was trampled by many feet, and littered with fragments, of iron and wood hurled from the demolished cars. The dead lay here and there, grotesquely sprawling where they fell. The dying moaned appeals for aid or, speechless, rolled their heads from side to side and writhed in agony. Everywhere there was blood and suffering and chaos."
>
> —*Tennessean*, June 10, 1918

They asked local butchers to come help manage the gore and horror. Still five
unidentified African American women and three unidentified African American
men destroyed beyond recognition. The railroad masonry abutments remain.
I touched them today.

***

I went on a first date last Thursday. We both leaned into each other's mouths
like two tipped tulips and just kissed each other at a bar called Answer as if that was
an answer—it wasn't. But it was instinctual, sudden and all pleasure. We kissed
all the way down Murphy Road, walking back to our cars, constellation of our juicy
hands everywhere. We kissed and groped, and I stopped obsessively thinking
about death for a few moments, maybe even for a whole evening, which was
the length of a tercet, an envoi sustained
with pleasure reaching for Black desire,
reaching for the transcendence of pain,   if possible. Is it possible?

Li-Young Lee

From Blossoms

From blossoms comes
this brown paper bag of peaches
we bought from the boy
at the bend in the road where we turned toward
signs painted *Peaches*.

From laden boughs, from hands,
from sweet fellowship in the bins,
comes nectar at the roadside, succulent
peaches we devour, dusty skin and all,
comes the familiar dust of summer, dust we eat.

O, to take what we love inside,
to carry within us an orchard, to eat
not only the skin, but the shade,
not only the sugar, but the days, to hold
the fruit in our hands, adore it, then bite into
the round jubilance of peach.

There are days we live
as if death were nowhere
in the background; from joy
to joy to joy, from wing to wing,
from blossom to blossom to
impossible blossom, to sweet impossible blossom.

Terrance Hayes

At Pegasus

They are like those crazy women
  who tore Orpheus
    when he refused to sing,

these men grinding
  in the strobe & black lights
    of Pegasus. All shadow & sound.

"I'm just here for the music,"
  I tell the man who asks me
    to the floor. But I have held

a boy on my back before.
  Curtis & I used to leap
    barefoot into the creek; dance

among maggots & piss,
  beer bottles & tadpoles
    slippery as sperm;

we used to pull off our shirts,
  & slap music into our skin.
    He wouldn't know me now

at the edge of these lovers' gyre,
  glitter & steam, fire,
    bodies blurred sexless

by the music's spinning light.
  A young man slips his thumb
    into the mouth of an old one,

& I am not that far away.
  The whole scene raw & delicate
    as Curtis's foot gashed

on a sunken bottle shard.
  They press hip to hip,
    each breathless as a boy

carrying a friend on his back.
  The foot swelling green
    as the sewage in that creek.

We never went back.
  But I remember his weight
    better than I remember

my first kiss.
  These men know something
    I used to know.

How could I not find them
  beautiful, the way they dive & spill
    into each other,

the way the dance floor
  takes them,
    wet & holy in its mouth.

Sharon Olds

Full Summer

I paused, and paused, over your body,
to feel the current of desire pull
and pull through me. Our hair was still wet,
mine like knotted wrack, it fell
across you as I paused, a soaked coil
around your glans. When one of your hairs
dried, it lifted like a bare nerve.
On the beach, above us, a cloud had appeared
in the clear air, a clockwise loop
coming in out of nothing, now the skin of your scrotum
moved like a live being, an animal,
I began to lick you, the foreskin lightly
stuck in one spot, like a petal, I love
to free it—just so—in joy,
and to sip from the little crying lips
at the tip. Then there was no more pausing,
nor was this the taker,
some new one came
and sucked, and up from where I had been hiding I was
drawn in a heavy spiral out of matter
over into another world
I had thought I would have to die to reach.

José Antonio Rodríguez

Men's Sexual-Trauma Support Group

It's less about talking
And more about the physical response,
The facilitator said. We sat in a circle
On foldout chairs and looked at the shuffling feet,
Imagined trusting someone else
With one's body. What would that be like?
The question I may have read in their glances.
Hard to say, busy as I was recalling
Hugging a friend after the long absence,
Or lifting the weighted bar off my chest at the gym
While my spotter traced its rise.
So that was part of the good feeling,
His body telling mine, I will not hurt you
Nor let you be hurt here now.
Hypervigilance, said the facilitator,
Comes after the freeze response,
No longer necessary and yet persistent.
I think I've gone through life
Observing it rather than living it,
I said almost at hour's end.
Wow, someone responded, I never had the words.
And I didn't have the nerve to say
That I'd made it my mission to find
All the words, to fill every room with them,
Let them fall over us, the faithful and the faithless,
Like balloons, like confetti, like glitter
Landing with the gentlest touch.

Paul Guest

Theories of Revenge

I think about the man who must be dead
by now and his undifferentiated son
and how they sat beside one another
that morning I nearly died in their yard.
I never learned his name, hair color,
where he went to church if he did,
and this morning I'm thinking
about the ethics of giving him a minor limp.
Some old wound that healed
wrong in another life. Tendon
that snapped in a filthy alley in San Juan.
1967. The light was different,
then, because the sun was.
Everything was. Years before my birth.
Years before Elvis died
on the toilet, his body ruined and ruptured,
and even though I grew up
in Tennessee I've never been to Graceland.
There is so much in life to regret.
To desire unto pain. To ignore, also.
There I lay in the weeds
of the ditch like garbage,
my body harmed forever,
though nobody then would really believe it,
and I felt little: some ache,
but mostly nothing, a spooky lack of weight
on the summer-hot ground.
I think there was panic
in the air above me like a ghost
and I struggled to breathe.
Do not move me or pick me up or touch me,
I begged the old man.
Something is wrong. Something was
wrong with the bicycle

and now inside me was something terrible
and lasting and final
and I think I wanted it all to be a bad dream.
The way my head fell over
when they stood me up. The horror when I collapsed.
There was no blood anywhere.
No visible wound. Just a boy in yellow surrounded by strangers.

Sarah Ghazal Ali

My Faith Gets Grime Under Its Nails

قل—SAY, HE IS ALLAH, THE ONE

I confess to sleeping coiled on my night-
blue prayer mat

more often than I stand bent in rukū.

Even when I posture piety
I blink steady, lashes keeping count of the hand-
knotted flowers fringing the rug

rather than God's pristine names.

The places I've prayed—elevators, Victoria's Secret
fitting room, the muck-slick meadow after rain—

will testify for or against me,
spilling through my Book of Deeds

in ink of blood or honeyed milk.

قل—SAY, I SEEK REFUGE IN THE LORD OF MANKIND

My faith is feminine, breasted
and irregularly bleeding

My faith gets grime under its nails

unburies maybe-mothers
to suckle them sacred. I believe
what I can't leave. I eat
hand-slaughtered beef

spared of pain. I laugh about the banyan tree

in Khyber chained by a drunk British officer
convinced it lurched toward him. I pull up a picture
online, show my mother the roses
planted neatly around it,

the rusted shackles no one dares remove

قل—SAY, I SEEK REFUGE WITH THE LORD OF DAWN

Once a month blood roams
like mint over immaculate grass,

the adhan trills from my arboreal center.

Though excused, I wake
before the white thread of day-
break to open my window,

let the angels in

to spectate the ache
and erase a sin for every devoted cramp.
Lord, you pardon my pain.
Lord, I parable my name.
As best as I can

I am raising my hands—

قل—SAY, O DISBELIEVERS

I read my char qul, cup my hands and blow.
I misremember and enter with the wrong foot
first. A woman crowned

holy is a calamity worth repeating.

Eve languished
motherless among rotting cores,
the sweet stench of fruit flies
at last shown their purpose.

What wilt, what putrefaction

of her will to wonder. I wonder how
to hallow the women I've sprung from.
I haven't begot a thing but inherited
wounds, I can't help but bear

what barely belongs to me.

Charles Wright

As Our Bodies Rise, Our Names Turn Into Light

The sky unrolls like a rug,
                                        unwelcoming, gun-grey,
Over the Blue Ridge.
Mothers are calling their children in,
                                                            mellifluous syllables, floating sounds.
The traffic shimmies and settles back.

The doctor has filled his truck with leaves
Next door, and a pair of logs.
Salt stones litter the street.
The snow falls and the wind drops.
How strange to have a name, any name, on this poor earth.

January hunkers down,
                                    the icicle deep in her throat—
The days become longer, the nights ground bitter and cold,
Single grain by single grain
Everything flows toward structure,
                                                      last ache in the ache for God.

Thomas James

Mummy of a Lady Named Jemutesonekh

XXI Dynasty

My body holds its shape. The genius is intact.
Will I return to Thebes? In that lost country
The eucalyptus trees have turned to stone.
Once, branches nudged me, dropping swollen blossoms,
And passionflowers lit my father's garden.
Is it still there, that place of mottled shadow,
The scarlet flowers breathing in the darkness?

I remember how I died. It was so simple!
One morning the garden faded. My face blacked out.
On my left side they made the first incision.
They washed my heart and liver in palm wine—
My lungs were two dark fruit they stuffed with spices.
They smeared my innards with a sticky unguent
And sealed them in a crock of alabaster.

My brain was next. A pointed instrument
Hooked it through my nostrils, strand by strand.
A voice swayed over me. I paid no notice.
For weeks my body swam in sweet perfume.
I came out scoured. I was skin and bone.
They lifted me into the sun again
And packed my empty skull with cinnamon.

They slit my toes; a razor gashed my fingertips.
Stitched shut at last, my limbs were chaste and valuable,
Stuffed with paste of cloves and wild honey.
My eyes were empty, so they filled them up,
Inserting little nuggets of obsidian.
A basalt scarab wedged between my breasts
Replaced the tinny music of my heart.

Hands touched my sutures. I was so important!
They oiled my pores, rubbing a fragrance in.
An amber gum oozed down to soothe my temples.
I wanted to sit up. My skin was luminous,
Frail as the shadow of an emerald.
Before I learned to love myself too much,
My body wound itself in spools of linen.

Shut in my painted box, I am a precious object.
I wear a wooden mask. These are my eyelids,
Two flakes of bronze, and here is my new mouth,
Chiseled with care, guarding its ruby facets.
I will last forever. I am not impatient—
My skin will wait to greet its old complexions.
I'll lie here till the world swims back again.

When I come home the garden will be budding,
White petals breaking open, clusters of night flowers,
The far-off music of a tambourine.
A boy will pace among the passionflowers,
His eyes no longer two bruised surfaces.
I'll know the mouth of my young groom, I'll touch
His hands. Why do people lie to one another?

Carrie Fountain

The Jungle

In motherhood I begin
to celebrate my own

smallest accomplishments,
as when I wake to find

I've slept through the night
and I feel a little healed

because sleeping is something
I didn't learn how to do until

I was an adult and had to read
a book about it because, I've

always liked to joke, I was
raised by wolves. *I was raised*

by wolves was, in fact, the very
joke I made in explaining

to a fellow mom as the children's
theater went dark that, like my own

young son, I was seeing *The Jungle*
Book for the first time. I don't

even know what it's about, I said.
I was sort of raised by wolves,

I said and laughed, and then
the curtain went up and I was

shocked, of course, to find
The Jungle Book is about a boy

who was raised by wolves,
and I am shocked again now,

having just googled it, to find
the number one query

associated with Rudyard
Kipling is: *Is the Jungle Book*

a real story? People are dumb
is what I was thinking, I admit,

when I read that, but then
I clicked and clicked and found

that—oh my god—*The Jungle*
Book is based on the story

of a feral boy found running
on all fours alongside a wolf

in the Indian jungle, which is
funny to me because *feral*

is the word that has always come
to mind when I think of the boys

I grew up with: those feral boys
who moved through the world

with the ease afforded to those
who didn't give two shits

about anything, who'd empty
beer cans in seconds, wrap cars

around poles, all the while joking
about fucking each other's

mother. They were feral
in the desert shooting guns out

by the airport. They were feral
on their skateboards in the Whata-

burger parking lot. They were feral
because they were allowed

to be, and eventually we'd all
get in trouble for what they'd been

doing, even us girls who—what did
we do all that time while the boys

were fighting and spitting
and calling us whores? I don't

know. We were talking to each
other, I guess, which is how we

became human. But no—no.
Those boys weren't feral. Those boys

were typical. They'd been born
knowing the world would be theirs

long after they'd grown bored
of nihilism and turned their attention

to capital, became men, became man-
kind, the kind of men who'd ruin

something if it meant they got to
keep it, who'd kill something

if it meant they could see it up close,
maintain the illusion of having

owned it, having earned it, even,
who'd track a boy and a wolf

through the jungle for days until
finally they had them trapped

inside their own den. When those
men found they couldn't lure

the boy out with words, they forced
him out with smoke. And when

the boy finally stepped out into
the sunlight those men captured

him, bound him, and when the wolf
who was the boy's mother came

following close behind, the way,
at intermission, I followed my own

son, who is by now too old
to come with me into the women's

room, to the very threshold
of the men's room door—when she

came out behind him, they shot her.

Denis Johnson

Now

Whatever the foghorns are
the voices of feels terrible
tonight, just terrible, and here
by the window that looks out
on the waters but is blind, I
have been sleeping,
but I am awake now.
In the night I watch
how the little lights
of boats come out
to us and are lost again
in the fog wallowing on the sea:
it is as if in that absence not many
but a single light gestures
and diminishes like meaning
through speech, negligently
adance to the calling
of the foghorns like the one
note they lend from voice
to voice. And so does my life tremble,
and when I turn from the window
and from the sea's grief, the room
fills with a dark
lushness and foliage nobody
will ever be plucked from,
and the feelings I have
must never be given speech.
Darkness, my name is Denis Johnson,
and I am almost ready to
confess it is not some awful
misunderstanding that has carried
me here, my arms full of the ghosts
of flowers, to kneel at your feet;
almost ready to see

how at each turning I chose
this way, this place and this verging
of ocean on earth with the horns claiming
I can keep on if only I step
where I cannot breathe. My coat
is leprosy and my dagger
is a lie; must I
shed them? Do I have
to end my life in order
to begin? Music, you are light.
Agony, you are only what tips
me from moment to moment, light
to light and word to word,
and I am here at the waters
because in this space between spaces
where nothing speaks,
I am what it says.

Franz Wright

The Only Animal

The only animal that commits suicide
went for a walk in the park,
basked on a hard bench
in the first star,
traveled to the edge of space
in an armchair
while company quietly
talked, and abruptly
returned,
the room empty

The only animal that cries,
that takes off its clothes
and reports to the mirror, the one
and only animal
that brushes its own teeth?

somewhere
the only animal that smokes a cigarette,
that lies down and flies backward in time,
that rises and walks to a book
and looks up a word
heard the telephone ringing
in the darkness downstairs and decided
to answer no more.

And I understand,
too well: how many times
have I made the decision to dwell
from now on
in the hour of my death
(the space I took up here
scarlessly closing like water)
and said I'm never coming back,
and yet

this morning
I stood once again
in this world,
the garden
ark and vacant
tomb of what
I can't imagine,
between twin eternities,
some sort of wings,
more or less equidistantly
exiled from both,
hovering in the dreaming called
being awake, where
You gave me
in secret one thing
to perceive, the
tall blue starry
strangeness of being
here at all.

You gave us each in secret one thing to perceive.

Furless now, upright, My banished
and experimental
child

You said, though your own heart condemn you

I do not condemn you.

Ross White

Quae Nocent Saepe Docent

My bow-legs crossed, I sat before someone I thought the great teacher.
His whole body a fist, he said, "Pain is the great teacher."

As sun rejects moon, as water rejects fire, one must reject a notion first
if one is ever to embrace it. The flower of denial, perhaps, the great teacher?

I wandered the museums of terra cotta soldiers and the mansions
of silence. I asked the ronin where I might find the great teacher.

I sent my dream-self to the rounded hovels at the edge of imagination.
I asked all the creatures in the dreaming where I might find the great teacher.

I learned to see the world through the eye of a needle, to shape sticks,
to sing mourning songs. I thought myself the envy of the great teacher.

But stone grew around my feet, and held me fast as I became stone.
Then I believed for some years that humility was the great teacher.

In autumn evening, the outline of a woman broke the purple horizon.
She looked at me with such pity, and asked if I had found the great teacher.

My ruin forgotten, I thawed. I built us a canoe, I painted figurines of ronin as gifts.
Her delight was rose-petal. I abandoned my search for the great teacher.

One cannot know incompletion until completed. Newly in love,
what need had I for the counsel of the great teacher?

It never occurred to me that I might undress my beloved and discover
the white blooms of scar across her back, shadows of the great teacher.

Cole Swenson

Stairs & Windows

Something happening on a spiral stair spirals the air there, and the green out the window gives in to the swirl, turning into fall, and a gust of falling leaves bursts in through the open window, spinning down through the stairwell just as the stairs themselves are winding their way upward.

The stairs, again spiral, and beyond them, the window, which again is open, and so a breeze follows that spiral downward, revolving the window on its vertical axis, as well as the person out there on the sidewalk, reflected in it, who is now heading off in the opposite direction.

That stair where you never expected it—up the core of a pear, for instance, or, suddenly, there instead of your little finger, and now responsible for the future.

Harryette Mullen

Sleeping with the Dictionary

I beg to dicker with my silver-tongued companion, whose lips are ready to read my shining gloss. A versatile partner, conversant and well-versed in the verbal art, the dictionary is not averse to the solitary habits of the curiously wide-awake reader. In the dark night's insomnia, the book is a stimulating sedative, awakening my tired imagination to the hypnagogic trance of language. Retiring to the canopy of the bedroom, turning on the bedside light, taking the big dictionary to bed, clutching the unabridged bulk, heavy with the weight of all the meanings between these covers, smoothing the thin sheets, thick with accented syllables—all are exercises in the conscious regimen of dreamers, who toss words on their tongues while turning illuminated pages. To go through all these motions and procedures, groping in the dark for an alluring word, is the poet's nocturnal mission. Aroused by myriad possibilities, we try out the most perverse positions in the practice of our nightly act, the penetration of the denotative body of the work. Any exit from the logic of language might be an entry in a symptomatic dictionary. The alphabetical order of this ample block of knowledge might render a dense lexicon of lucid hallucinations. Beside the bed, a pad lies open to record the meandering of migratory words. In the rapid eye movement of the poet's night vision, this dictum can be decoded, like the secret acrostic of a lover's name.

Robert Creeley

The Language

Locate *I*
love you some-
where in

teeth and
eyes, bite
it but

take care not
to hurt, you
want so

much so
little. Words
say everything.

I
love you
again,

then what
is emptiness
for. To

fill, fill.
I heard words
and words full

of holes
aching. Speech
is a mouth.

Rae Armantrout

The Way

Card in pew pocket
announces,
"I am here."

I made only one statement
because of a bad winter.

Grease is the word; grease
is the way

I am feeling.
Real life emergencies or

flubbing behind the scenes.

As a child,
I was abandoned

in a story
made of trees.

Here's the small
gasp

of this clearing
come "upon" "again"

Stanley Kunitz

The Layers

I have walked through many lives,
some of them my own,
and I am not who I was,
though some principle of being
abides, from which I struggle
not to stray.
When I look behind,
as I am compelled to look
before I can gather strength
to proceed on my journey,
I see the milestones dwindling
toward the horizon
and the slow fires trailing
from the abandoned camp-sites,
over which scavenger angels
wheel on heavy wings.
Oh, I have made myself a tribe
out of my true affections,
and my tribe is scattered!
How shall the heart be reconciled
to its feast of losses?
In a rising wind
the manic dust of my friends,
those who fell along the way,
bitterly stings my face.
Yet I turn, I turn,
exulting somewhat,
with my will intact to go
wherever I need to go,
and every stone on the road
precious to me.
In my darkest night,
when the moon was covered
and I roamed through wreckage,

a nimbus-clouded voice
directed me:
"Live in the layers,
not on the litter."
Though I lack the art
to decipher it,
no doubt the next chapter
in my book of transformations
is already written.
I am not done with my changes.

Cleopatra Mathis

Willful

All day, I fought myself, every word
invented to fit the seam of my gaze—
then fell asleep in late sun

that woke me, fur-mouthed and burned.
I'm not ready for evening
in the bordering woods, my walk where bears prowl

through dusk. I chant my willful spell,
Bears in the woods, Bears in the woods, Praise be,
Bears! I'm afraid they'll catch me anyway—

they look too much like stumps
in the looming shade. Yesterday, I turned
to see the fisher's black flash cross my path.

Innards are all she eats: five house cats
stolen for her litter just last week.
It's the closed summer dark

that sends me back to the roadside light,
where I name the easy *furled pods of milkweed /*
babies bound in fuzz...

And like a talisman, a thrush somewhere
starts up: a moment made beautiful
by singing, and something else

starts dying. Flushed, nesting grouse
scramble out in a rising tangle.
Struggle shakes the wall of leaves, the screen

of chlorophyll and spores, chemical cells,
            the on-going breathing air.
I can't look, hurrying up the road

to reach the field, expansive, benign,
            although it is nothing I want,
calling as it does to that cultivated thing, my heart.

Spencer Reece

ICU

For A.J. Verdelle

Those mornings I traveled north on I-91,
passing below the basalt cliff of East Rock
where the elms discussed their genealogies.
I was a chaplain at Hartford Hospital,
took the Myers-Briggs with Sister Margaret,
learned I was an *I* drawn to *E*s.
In small group I said, "I do not like it,
the way so many young black men die in the ER
shot, unrecognized, their gurneys stripped,
their belongings catalogued and unclaimed."
In the neonatal ICU, newborns breathed,
blue, spider-delicate in a nest of tubes.
A Sunday of themselves, their tissue purpled,
their eyelids the film on old water in a well,
their faces resigned in plastic attics,
their skin mottled mildewed wallpaper.
It is correct to love even at the wrong time.
On rounds, the newborns eyed me, each one
like Orpheus in his dark hallway, saying:
I knew I would find you, I knew I would lose you.

Lucille Clifton

1994

i was leaving my fifty-eighth year
when a thumb of ice
stamped itself hard near my heart

you have your own story
you know about the fears the tears
the scar of disbelief

you know that the saddest lies
are the ones we tell ourselves
you know how dangerous it is

to be born with breasts
you know how dangerous it is
to wear dark skin

i was leaving my fifty-eighth year
when i woke into the winter
of a cold and mortal body

thin icicles hanging off
the one mad nipple weeping

have we not been good children
did we not inherit the earth

but you must know all about this
from your own shivering life

Sarah Holland-Batt

The Gift

In the garden, my father sits in his wheelchair
garlanded by summer hibiscus
like a saint in a seventeenth-century cartouche.
A flowering wreath buzzes around his head—
passionate red. He holds the gift of death
in his lap: small, oblong, wrapped in black.
He has been waiting seventeen years to open it
and is impatient. When I ask how he is
my father cries. His crying comes as a visitation,
the body squeezing tears from his ducts tenderly
as a nurse measuring drops of calamine
from an amber bottle, as a teen at the car wash
wringing a chamois of suds. It is a kind of miracle
to see my father weeping this freely, weeping
for what is owed him. *How are you*? I ask again
because his answer depends on an instant's microclimate,
his moods bloom and retreat like an anemone
as the cold currents whirl around him—
crying one minute, sedate the next.
But today my father is disconsolate.
I'm having a bad day, he says, and tries again.
I'm having a bad year. I'm having a bad decade.
I hate myself for noticing his poetry—the triplet
that should not be beautiful to my ear
but is. Day, year, decade—scale of awful economy.
I want to give him his present but it is not mine
to give. We sit as if mother and son on Christmas Eve
waiting for midnight to tick over, anticipating
the moment we can open his present together—
first my father holding it up to his ear and shaking it,
then me helping him peel back the paper,
the weight of his death knocking,

and once the box is unwrapped it will be mine,
I will carry the gift of his death endlessly,
every day I will know it opening in me.

David Kirby

Get Up, Please

The two musicians pour forth their souls abroad
in such an ecstasy as to charm the audience
like none I've ever seen before, and when
they finish, they rise and hug each other,
and then the tabla player bends down
and touches the feet of the santoor player in an obvious gesture

of respect, but what does it mean? I don't find out
until the next day at the Econolodge in Tifton, GA,
where I stop on my way home after the concert
and ask Mrs. Patel, the owner, if she has ever heard
of these two musicians or knows
anything about the tabla and the santoor and especially the latter,

which looks like the love child of a typewriter
and a hammered dulcimer only with a lot of extra wires
and tuning posts, and she doesn't seem to understand
my questions, though when I ask her about one person touching
the other's feet and then bend down
to show her, she lights up and says, "It means he thinks the other

is a god. My children do this before they go off
to school in the morning, as though to say, 'Mummy,
you are a god to us,'" and I look at her
for a second and then surprise us both when I say, "Oh, Mrs. Patel!"
and burst into tears, because I think,
first, of my own dead parents and then of little Lakshmi and Padma

Patel going off to their classes in Tift County schools,
the one a second-grader who is studying homophones
("I see the sea") and the other of whom is in the fourth
grade, where she must master long division with
its cruel insistence on numbers lined
up under one another with exacting precision and then crawling

toward the page's bottom as you, the divider, subtract
and divide again and again, all the while recording
on the top line an answer that grows increasingly
lengthy as you fret and chew the tip of your pencil
and persevere, though before they grab
their books and lunch boxes and pile onto the bus, they take time

to touch Mrs. Patel's feet and Mr. Patel's as well,
assuming there is such a person. Later my friend
Avni tells me you touch the feet of your elders
to respect the distance they have traveled
and the earth they have touched, and you
say "namaste"not because you take yoga at that little place

on the truck route between the t-shirt store
and the strip club but because it means "I bow
to the light within you," and often the people being
bowed to will stoop down and collect you as if to say
"You too are made of the same light!"
Reader, if your parents are alive, think of them now, of all the gods

whose feet you never touched or touched enough.
And if not your parents, then someone else.
You know someone like this, right? Someone who belongs
to the "mighty dead," as Keats called them.
Don't you wish that person were here now
so you could touch their feet and whisper, "You are my god"?

I can't imagine Keats saying, "You too are made
of the same light," though I can see him saying,
as he did to Fanny Brawne, "I have been astonished
that Men could die Martyrs for religion—I have
shudder'd at it—I shudder no more—I could
be martyr'd for my Religion—Love is my religion—I could die for that—

I could die for you." My own feet have touched
the earth nearly three times as long as Keats's did,
and I'm hardly the oldest person
I know. So let this poem brush across the feet of anyone
who reads it. Poetry is
my religion—well, I wouldn't die for it. I'd live for it, though.

Maggie Smith

Good Bones

Life is short, though I keep this from my children.
Life is short, and I've shortened mine
in a thousand delicious, ill-advised ways,
a thousand deliciously ill-advised ways
I'll keep from my children. The world is at least
fifty percent terrible, and that's a conservative
estimate, though I keep this from my children.
For every bird there is a stone thrown at a bird.
For every loved child, a child broken, bagged,
sunk in a lake. Life is short and the world
is at least half terrible, and for every kind
stranger, there is one who would break you,
though I keep this from my children. I am trying
to sell them the world. Any decent realtor,
walking you through a real shithole, chirps on
about good bones: This place could be beautiful,
right? You could make this place beautiful.

Natalie Scenters-Zapico

Buen Esqueleto

Life is short, and I tell this to mis hijas.
Life is short, & I show them how to talk
to police without opening the door, how
to leave the social security number blank
on the exam, I tell this to mis hijas.
This world tells them I hate you every day
& I don't keep this from mis hijas
because of the bus driver who kicks them out
onto the street for fare evasion. Because I love
mis hijas, I keep them from men who'd knock
their heads together just to hear the chime.
Life is short & the world is terrible. I know
no kind strangers in this country who aren't
sisters a desert away, & I don't keep this
from mis hijas. It's not my job to sell
them the world, but to keep them safe
in case I get deported. Our first
landlord said with a bucket of bleach
the mold would come right off. He shook
mis hijas, said they had good bones
for hard work. *Mi'jas, could we make this place*
beautiful? I tried to make this place beautiful.

(After "Good Bones" by Maggie Smith)

Charif Shanahan

Trace Evidence

When I say *But mother, Black or not Black,*
Of course you are polyethnic, your look does not change
Though it does harden, a drying clay bust
Abandoned or deliberately incomplete,
All the features carved in
Except the eyes. *What I'm trying—*
I mean—You are an Arab, yes,
By culture, by language, and in part by blood; by blood
You are also Black African—and when, then, I say
And also probably a fair amount of European, too—the lights,
Though we're standing at the corner of 195th and Jerome,

Turn up somehow

Tracing an outline of you onto the armory's sharp red brick, the El
Barreling up from the tunnel like a surge of magma reaching
For air and as I wait for it to pass so that you can
Hear me again, so that I can hear myself at last
Say *But here, for me, that doesn't exactly matter. Don't you see—?*
Your face hangs on the *fair* of *fair amount*—heavy drops
Of oil, or old rain, falling onto us from the tracks—almost willing away
The layer of long-dead men flattened onto it, and the desperate
Rest of you, until I say with my looking
Through the unbearable human noise, *My darling sweet mother, it is*
Fine, it is fine. For us here now I will be the first of our line.

R. S. Thomas

Threshold

I emerge from the mind's
cave into the worse darkness
outside, where things pass and
the Lord is in none of them.

I have heard the still, small voice
and it was that of the bacteria
demolishing my cosmos. I
have lingered too long on

this threshold, but where can I go?
To look back is to lose the soul
I was leading upwards towards
the light. To look forward? Ah,

what balance is needed at
the edges of such an abyss.
I am alone on the surface
of a turning planet. What

to do but, like Michelangelo's
Adam, put my hand
out into unknown space,
hoping for the reciprocating touch?

William Stafford

Ask Me

Some time when the river is ice ask me
mistakes I have made. Ask me whether
what I have done is my life. Others
have come in their slow way into
my thought, and some have tried to help
or to hurt: ask me what difference
their strongest love or hate has made.

I will listen to what you say.
You and I can turn and look
at the silent river and wait. We know
the current is there, hidden; and there
are comings and goings from miles away
that hold the stillness exactly before us.
What the river says, that is what I say.

Ruth Stone

Metamorphosis

Now I am old, all I want to do is try;
But when I was young, if it wasn't easy I let it lie,
Learning through my pores instead,
And it did neither of us any good.

For now she is gone who slept away my life,
And I am ignorant who inherited,
Though the head has grown so lively that I laugh,
"Come look, come stomp, come listen to the drum."

I see more now than then; but she who had my eyes
Closed them in happiness, and wrapped the dark
In her arms and stole my life away,
Singing in dreams of what was sure to come.

I see it perfectly, except the beast
Fumbles and falters, until the others wince.
Everything shimmers and glitters and shakes with unbearable longing,
The dancers who cannot sleep, and the sleepers who cannot dance.

Rita Dove

Canary

for Michael S. Harper

Billie Holiday's burned voice
had as many shadows as lights,
a mournful candelabra against a sleek piano,
the gardenia her signature under that ruined face.

(Now you're cooking, drummer to bass,
magic spoon, magic needle.
Take all day if you have to
with your mirror and your bracelet of song.)

Fact is, the invention of women under siege
has been to sharpen love in the service of myth.

If you can't be free, be a mystery.

Robert Hass

Meditation at Lagunitas

All the new thinking is about loss.
In this it resembles all the old thinking.
The idea, for example, that each particular erases
the luminous clarity of a general idea. That the clown-
faced woodpecker probing the dead sculpted trunk
of that black birch is, by his presence,
some tragic falling off from a first world
of undivided light. Or the other notion that,
because there is in this world no one thing
to which the bramble of *blackberry* corresponds,
a word is elegy to what it signifies.
We talked about it late last night and in the voice
of my friend, there was a thin wire of grief, a tone
almost querulous. After a while I understood that,
talking this way, everything dissolves: *justice*,
pine, *hair*, *woman*, *you* and *I*. There was a woman
I made love to and I remembered how, holding
her small shoulders in my hands sometimes,
I felt a violent wonder at her presence
like a thirst for salt, for my childhood river
with its island willows, silly music from the pleasure boat,
muddy places where we caught the little orange-silver fish
called *pumpkinseed*. It hardly had to do with her.
Longing, we say, because desire is full
of endless distances. I must have been the same to her.
But I remember so much, the way her hands dismantled bread,
the thing her father said that hurt her, what
she dreamed. There are moments when the body is as numinous
as words, days that are the good flesh continuing.
Such tenderness, those afternoons and evenings,
saying *blackberry*, *blackberry*, *blackberry*.

B. H. Fairchild

Beauty

> *Therefore,*
> *Their sons grow suicidally beautiful…*
>
> —James Wright, "Autumn Begins in Martin's Ferry, Ohio"

I.

We are at the Bargello in Florence, and she says,
what are you thinking? and I say, *beauty*, thinking
of how very far we are now from the machine shop
and the dry fields of Kansas, the treeless horizons
of slate skies and the muted passions of roughnecks
and scrabble farmers drunk and romantic enough
to weep more or less silently at the darkened end
of the bar out of, what else, loneliness, meaning
the ache of thwarted desire, of, in a word, *beauty*,
or rather its absence, and it occurs to me again
that no male member of my family has ever used
this word in my hearing or anyone else's except
in reference, perhaps, to a new pickup or dead deer.
This insight, this backward vision, first came to me
as a young man as some weirdness of the air waves
slipped through the static of our new Motorola
with a discussion of *beauty* between Robert Penn Warren
and Paul Weiss at Yale College. We were in Kansas
eating barbecue-flavored potato chips and waiting
for *Father Knows Best* to float up through the snow
of rural TV in 1963. I felt transported, stunned.
Here were two grown men discussing "beauty"
seriously and with dignity as if they and the topic
were as normal as normal topics of discussion
between men such as soybean prices or why
the commodities market was a sucker's game
or Oklahoma football or Gimpy Neiderland
almost dying from his hemorrhoid operation.

They were discussing beauty and tossing around
allusions to Plato and Aristotle and someone
named Pater, and they might be homosexuals.
That would be a natural conclusion, of course,
since here were two grown men talking about "beauty"
instead of scratching their crotches and cursing
the goddamned government trying to run everybody's
business. Not a beautiful thing, that. The government.
Not beautiful, though a man would not use that word.
One time my Uncle Ross from California called my mom's
Sunday dinner centerpiece "lovely" and my father
left the room, clearly troubled by the word *lovely*
coupled probably with the very idea of California
and the fact that my Uncle Ross liked to tap-dance.
The light from the venetian blinds, the autumn,
silver Kansas light laving the table that Sunday,
is what I recall now because it was beautiful,
though I of course would not have said so then, *beautiful*,
as so many moments forgotten but later remembered
come back to us in slants and pools and uprisings of light,
beautiful in itself, but more beautiful mingled
with memory, the light leaning across my mother's
carefully set table, across the empty chair
beside my Uncle Ross, the light filtering down
from the green plastic slats in the roof of the machine shop
where I worked with my father so many afternoons,
standing or crouched in pools of light and sweat with men
who knew the true meaning of labor and money and other
hard, true things and did not, did not ever, use the word, *beauty*.

II.

Late November, shadows gather in the shop's north end,
and I'm watching Bobby Sudduth do piece work on the Hobbs.
He fouls another cut, *motherfucker, fucking bitch machine*,
and starts over, sloppy, slow, about two joints away
from being fired, but he just doesn't give a shit.
He sets the bit again, white wrists flashing in the lamplight
and showing botched, blurred tattoos, both from a night

in Tijuana, and continues his sexual autobiography,
that's right, fucked my own sister, and I'll tell you, bud,
it wasn't bad. Later, in the Phillipines, the clap:
as far as I'm concerned, any man who hasn't had VD
just isn't a man. I walk away, knowing I have just heard
the dumbest remark ever uttered by man or animal.
The air around me hums in a dark metallic bass,
light spilling like grails of milk as someone opens
the mammoth shop door. A shrill, sullen truculence
blows in like dust devils, the hot wind nagging
my blousy overalls, and in the sideyard the winch truck
backfires and stalls. The sky yellows. Barn sparrows cry
in the rafters. That afternoon in Dallas Kennedy is shot.

Two weeks later sitting around on rotary tables
and traveling blocks whose bearings litter the shop floor
like huge eggs, we close our lunch boxes and lean back
with cigarettes and watch smoke and dust motes rise and drift
into sunlight. All of us have seen the newscasts,
photographs from *Life*, have sat there in our cavernous rooms,
assassinations and crowds flickering over our faces,
some of us have even dreamed it, sleeping through
the TV's drone and flutter, seen her arm reaching
across the lank body, black suits rushing in like moths,
and the long snake of the motorcade come to rest,
then the announcer's voice as we wake astonished in the dark.
We think of it now, staring at the tin ceiling like a giant screen,
what a strange goddamned country, as Bobby Sudduth
arches a wadded Fritos bag at the time clock and says,
Oswald, from that far, you got to admit, that shot was a beauty.

III.

The following summer. A black Corvette gleams like a slice
of onyx in the sideyard, driven there by two young men
who look like Marlon Brando and mention Hollywood
when Bobby asks where they're from. The foreman, my father,
has hired them because we're backed up with work, both shop
and yard strewn with rig parts, flat-bed haulers rumbling

in each day lugging damaged drawworks, and we are desperate.
The noise is awful, a gang of roughnecks from a rig
on down-time shouting orders, our floor hands knee-deep
in the drawwork's gears heating the frozen sleeves and bushings
with cutting torches until they can be hammered loose.
The iron shell bangs back like a drumhead. Looking
for some peace, I walk onto the pipe rack for a quick smoke,
and this is the way it begins for me, this memory,
this strangest of all memories of the shop and the men
who worked there, because the silence has come upon me
like the shadow of cranes flying overhead as they would
each autumn, like the quiet and imperceptible turning
of a season, the shop has grown suddenly still here
in the middle of the workday, and I turn to look
through the tall doors where the machinists stand now
with their backs to me, the lathes whining down together,
and in the shop's center I see them standing in a square
of light, the two men from California, as the welders
lift their black masks, looking up, and I see their faces first,
the expressions of children at a zoo, perhaps,
or after a first snow, as the two men stand naked,
their clothes in little piles on the floor as if they
are about to go swimming, and I recall how fragile
and pale their bodies seemed against the iron and steel
of the drill presses and milling machines and lathes.
I did not know the word, *exhibitionist*, then, and so
for a moment it seemed only a problem of memory,
that they had *forgotten* somehow where they were,
that this was not the locker room after the game,
that they were not taking a shower, that this was not
the appropriate place, and they would then remember,
and suddenly embarrassed, begin shyly to dress again.
But they did not, and in memory they stand frozen
and poised as two models in a drawing class,
of whom the finished sketch might be said, though not by me
nor any man I knew, to be beautiful, they stand there
forever, with the time clock ticking behind them,
time running on but not moving, like the white tunnel
of silence between the snap of the ball and the thunderclap

of shoulder pads that never seems to come and then
there it is, and I hear a quick intake of breath
on my right behind the Hobbs and it is Bobby Sudduth
with what I think now was not just anger but a kind
of terror on his face, an animal wildness
in the eyes and the jaw tight, making ropes in his neck
while in a long blur with his left hand raised and gripping
an iron file he is moving toward the men who wait
attentive and motionless as deer trembling in a clearing,
and instantly there is my father between Bobby
and the men as if he were waking them after a long sleep,
reaching out to touch the shoulder of the blonde one
as he says in a voice almost terrible in its gentleness,
its discretion, *you boys will have to leave now.*
He takes one look at Bobby who is shrinking back
into the shadows of the Hobbs, then walks quickly back
to his office at the front of the shop, and soon
the black Corvette with the orange California plates
is squealing onto Highway 54 heading west into the sun.

IV.

So there they are, as I will always remember them,
the men who were once fullbacks or tackles or guards
in their three-point stances knuckling into the mud,
hungry for high school glory and the pride of their fathers,
eager to *gallop terribly against each other's bodies*,
each man in his body looking out now at the nakedness
of a body like his, men who each autumn had followed
their fathers into the pheasant-rich fields of Kansas
and as boys had climbed down from the Allis-Chalmers
after plowing their first straight furrow, licking the dirt
from their lips, the hand of the father resting lightly
upon their shoulder, men who in the oven-warm winter
kitchens of Baptist households saw after a bath the body
of the father and felt diminished by it, who that same
winter in the abandoned schoolyard felt the odd intimacy
of their fist against the larger boy's cheekbone
but kept hitting, ferociously, and walked away

feeling for the first time the strength, the *abundance*,
of their own bodies. And I imagine the men
that evening after the strangest day of their lives,
after they have left the shop without speaking
and made the long drive home alone in their pickups,
I see them in their little white frame houses on the edge
of town adrift in the long silence of the evening turning
finally to their wives, touching without speaking the hair
which she has learned to let fall about her shoulders
at this hour of the night, lifting the white nightgown
from her body as she in turn unbuttons his work shirt
heavy with the sweat and grease of the day's labor until
they stand naked before each other and begin to touch
in a slow choreography of familiar gestures their bodies,
she touching his chest, his hand brushing her breasts,
and he does not say the word *beautiful* because
he cannot and never has, and she does not say it
because it would embarrass him or any other man
she has ever known, though it is precisely the word
I am thinking now as I stand before Donatello's *David*
with my wife touching my sleeve, *what are you thinking*?
and I think of the letter from my father years ago
describing the death of Bobby Sudduth, a single shot
from a twelve-gauge which he held against his chest,
the death of the heart, I suppose, *a kind of terrible beauty*,
as someone said of the death of Hart Crane, though that is
surely a perverse use of the word, and I was stunned then,
thinking of the damage men will visit upon their bodies,
what are you thinking? she asks again, and so I begin
to tell her about a strange afternoon in Kansas,
about something I have never spoken of, and we walk
to a window where the shifting light spreads a sheen
along the casement, and looking out, we see the city
blazing like miles of uncut wheat, the farthest buildings
taken in their turn, and the great dome, the way
the metal roof of the machine shop, I tell her,
would break into flame late on an autumn day, with such beauty.

Larry Levis

Winter Stars

My father once broke a man's hand
Over the exhaust pipe of a John Deere tractor. The man,
Rubén Vásquez, wanted to kill his own father
With a sharpened fruit knife, & he held
The curved tip of it, lightly, between his first
Two fingers, so it could slash
Horizontally, & with surprising grace,
Across a throat. It was like a glinting beak in a hand,
And, for a moment, the light held still
On those vines. When it was over,
My father simply went in & ate lunch, & then, as always,
Lay alone in the dark, listening to music.
He never mentioned it.

I never understood how anyone could risk his life,
Then listen to Vivaldi.

Sometimes, I go out into this yard at night,
And stare through the wet branches of an oak
In winter, & realize I am looking at the stars
Again. A thin haze of them, shining
And persisting.

It used to make me feel lighter, looking up at them.
In California, that light was closer.
In a California no one will ever see again,
My father is beginning to die. Something
Inside him is slowly taking back
Every word it ever gave him.
Now, if we try to talk, I watch my father
Search for a lost syllable as if it might
Solve everything, & though he can't remember, now,
The word for it, he is ashamed . . .
If you can think of the mind as a place continually

Visited, a whole city placed behind
The eyes, & shining, I can imagine, now, its end—
As when the lights go off, one by one,
In a hotel at night, until at last
All of the travelers will be asleep, or until
Even the thin glow from the lobby is a kind
Of sleep; & while the woman behind the desk
Is applying more lacquer to her nails,
You can almost believe that the elevator,
As it ascends, must open upon starlight.

I stand out on the street, & do not go in.
That was our agreement, at my birth.

And for years I believed
That what went unsaid between us became empty,
And pure, like starlight, & that it persisted.

I got it all wrong.
I wound up believing in words the way a scientist
Believes in carbon, after death.

Tonight, I'm talking to you, father, although
It is quiet here in the Midwest, where a small wind,
The size of a wrist, wakes the cold again—
Which may be all that's left of you & me.

When I left home at seventeen, I left for good.

That pale haze of stars goes on & on,
Like laughter that has found a final, silent shape
On a black sky. It means everything
It cannot say. Look, it's empty out there, & cold.
Cold enough to reconcile
Even a father, even a son.

Robert Hayden

Those Winter Sundays

Sundays too my father got up early
and put his clothes on in the blueblack cold,
then with cracked hands that ached
from labor in the weekday weather made
banked fires blaze. No one ever thanked him.

I'd wake and hear the cold splintering, breaking.
When the rooms were warm, he'd call,
and slowly I would rise and dress,
fearing the chronic angers of that house,

Speaking indifferently to him,
who had driven out the cold
and polished my good shoes as well.
What did I know, what did I know
of love's austere and lonely offices?

Vievee Francis

Taking It

for Gabby and Jen

I never remember the knuckles, though
his hand was bare, though their hands were bare.
I remember the impressions left on this skin, the
wilting and the welting. I don't remember the sound,
not one smack. I remember the falls, myself falling
to the floor or sidewalk, or against the brick wall
my head met after a push. There were many pushes.
Girls pushed but I punched. Pulled one
down by the hair and kneed her as my head bled.
Girls didn't punch until high school. I had always
punched. What kind of girl are you?
The kind who wants to live, I said, and I did want to
until I didn't anymore. But I wanted the leaving
to be on my terms, so I hit my father back.
He owned me like any good, country father. He
waited for a husband to tame what he couldn't corral,
to throw a rope like fingers 'round a neck.
When I missed a boy, fingerholds—I remember those,
and me making a fist wrongly, and punching
and I didn't mean to miss but to hit the line below the belly,
the beltline. W—— broke me in the snow
my first year North. I'm still afraid to say his name.
I wore shoes too thin for the weather (who had ever seen
such snow?) and had a Georgia lilt, like molasses
on a sore throat, sugared, raw, and he hated the sound of it.
He was black and I was black and I was so happy
to be in Detroit, and he aimed for my heart-
shaped mouth, my gapped teeth, my too-sweet tongue.
I felt the juvenile weight of him above me like snow after dark
falling steady and hard. I'm gone teach you to talk reg'lar,
and I stopped speaking at all. I kept my swollen mouth shut,
and a straight razor in my math book, and dreamt of a bat

cracking against his chest. A woman like me
with soft hands, not hands of the field, but
hands meant to stroke and soothe, needs a weapon,
so I studied The Art of War and watched boxing, and
where else was all this rage to go? Is this too dramatic?
Find another story. Find a lie. In love, body after body
fell beneath my own, though my own was broken,
and I made love like a sea creature, fluid as if boneless
though my bones would rattle if not for the fat I cherish.
Wouldn't you? And I grew to love the heavyweights,
myself with one in the ring. Imagine him punching
me, and punching me again, saying I'm sorry, so sorry,
to have to love you this way.

Natasha Trethewey

Incident

We tell the story every year—
how we peered from the windows, shades drawn—
though nothing really happened,
the charred grass now green again.

We peered from the windows, shades drawn,
at the cross trussed like a Christmas tree,
the charred grass still green. Then
we darkened our rooms, lit the hurricane lamps.

At the cross trussed like a Christmas tree,
a few men gathered, white as angels in their gowns.
We darkened our rooms and lit hurricane lamps,
the wicks trembling in their fonts of oil.

It seemed the angels had gathered, white men in their gowns.
When they were done, they left quietly. No one came.
The wicks trembled all night in their fonts of oil;
by morning the flames had all dimmed.

When they were done, the men left quietly. No one came.
Nothing really happened.
By morning all the flames had dimmed.
We tell the story every year.

Mosab Abu Toha

In the War: you and houses

You fight. You
die.
You'll never know who won or lost,
or if the war ever ended.

They didn't find a place to bury you.
They carried you on their shoulders,
wandered through the neighborhood,
stopped at your childhood school
and the old park.

The houses never saw you.
They've already packed their bags.
Dust has erected a tent in the corners.
Rust has landed with its worn-out clothes on the tap
and on the spoon.
It steals from the water its soft slide,
while you,
you sleep on moving sand.

Monica Youn

Detail of the Rice Chest

In the 2015 Korean film *The Throne,* the rice chest sits in the center of the vast, symmetrical courtyard of Changgyeonggung Palace.

The film is called *The Throne* in English; in Korean it is called *Sado.*

A Korean-speaking audience would be presumed to know in advance who Prince Sado was.

An English-speaking audience is presumed not to have this knowledge.

Although this is a historical film, for a Korean-speaking audience the well-known story functions as mythology, at the level of symbol.

For an English-speaking audience the unknown story functions as narrative, at the level of plot.

There is an "I" in this poem.

I know who Prince Sado is, I can read the Hangul word *Sado.* But I do not speak Korean.

I am a member of the English-speaking audience.

I know about Prince Sado from *The Memoirs of Lady Hyegyeong* (1804). But I know about *The Memoirs of Lady Hyegyeong* from Margaret Drabble's *The Red Queen* (2004).

Margaret Drabble's *The Red Queen* is about Lady Hyegyeong. But Lady Hyegyeong was never a queen, nor is she associated with the color red. The name is misleading.

The name of the film *The Throne* is also misleading. The film does not focus on the throne; it focuses on the rice chest.

Like a magnifying glass, the stone courtyard focuses the gaze on the rice chest. The gaze increases in intensity and heat.

July temperatures in Seoul average 84 degrees Fahrenheit, with average humidity of 78 percent.

I have been to Seoul in July, I have worn *hanbok* on a summer day, but only once.

I have never seen a rice chest.

The rice chest is a functional object and stands in contrast to the highly decorative architecture of the palace courtyard. Its plainness renders it inscrutable, impenetrable.

According to the website *Hanji Happenings*: "The solid rice chest was generally made of pine but never decorated as a reminder of the importance of its presence in the home." I learn from that statement that in Korean culture to be decorative is not to be important, and, conversely, that to be plain, inscrutable, is to be important. I do not know whether this is true.

According to the book *Things Korean,* the rice chest "always looks chock-full. There are always those four pillars at its corners which seem to be holding up a massive roof, as if this were some imposing religious edifice."

Because of its oversize lid, the rice chest appears top-heavy, charged with kinetic potential. With four small feet it seems to be crouching on its haunches, to be hunkering down.

"Hunker down" is a Scottish term that refers to squatting on the balls of one's feet, low to the ground but in readiness. It implies an apprehensive stasis, tense with the potential for sudden movement, poised to flee or to attack.

I have hunkered down, but only once.

Midway through the film, the rice chest is bound with thick rope, with a knotted webbing of four or five thicknesses of coarse, fibrous rope. The quantity of rope exceeds the function of the rope to such an extent that the rope binding seems decorative, symbolic.

I have been bound with rope, but only once.

There is something almost comic about such an excess of rope to bind a single imprisoned and dying man, the way there is something almost comic about a circle of guns pointed at a single unarmed man. I say almost comic rather than actually comic because, although these images provoke the same pent-up tension as suppressed laughter, I do not know who would find either of these images funny.

After it is bound, the lid of the rice chest is heaped with grass.

For a Korean-speaking audience, the grass-covered rice chest would resemble a traditional grassy burial mound, would evoke ancestral tombs, or even the prehistoric dolmens, which feature massive rocks perched on four small feet.

I have seen the grassy burial mounds of my ancestors, but only once.

For me, the rope-clad, grass-covered rice chest resembles a barbarian idol.

According to the Online Etymology Dictionary, the word "barbarian" originally comes from the Greek meaning any non-Greek and carries a derogatory connotation for those who speak a language different from one's own.

When I say "barbarian," it means I find the rice chest foreign, inscrutable, although it is Korean—Koreans speak a language different from my own.

In the film, the walls of the rice chest are made of thick planks, with chinks between them that admit slim shafts of light, drips of water.

But the walls of Korean rice chests are made of solid panels of wood. Planks with chinks between them would admit pests, especially insects, into the rice chest. Such a design would not be functional.

Partway through the film, we see a multilegged insect enter the rice chest through a chink between the boards. "We" here refers to both English-speaking and Korean-speaking audiences.

The single insect is followed by a horde of identical multilegged insects wriggling through the chinks in the walls. We understand the insects to be a hallucination of the dying Prince Sado. Their function is symbolic, the danger of allowing chinks in the walls.

In the film, through the chinks in the walls, Prince Sado is able to see and to speak to his dog and to his ten-year-old son, the Grand Heir.

But in fact these incidents never took place. They are not hallucinations but fabrications of the filmmakers just as the multilegged insects, the chinks in the walls of the rice chest are fabrications of the filmmakers.

The chinks allow the gaze to penetrate what would otherwise be impenetrable, to penetrate the inscrutable, barbaric figure of the rice chest, to reach the human inside.

In *A Midsummer Night's Dream,* which is familiar to both Korean- and English-speaking audiences, Tom Snout, a "rude mechanical," plays the part of a wall that features "a crannied hole or chink."

The joke is that a human being portrays an inhuman object, since only an inhuman object would feature such a chink. I do not know who would find this joke funny.

When asked to "Show me thy chink," Tom Snout holds up two fingers.

I have seen boys hold up two fingers. Calling me a chink, they would place their two fingers at the corners of their eyes, stretching their eyes into narrow slits through which it must have been difficult to see. They found this joke funny.

I have seen men hold up two fingers. They would use their tongues to penetrate the chink between their fingers, rendering the gesture obscene. The tongue thrust between the fingers reads as sexual, whereas an outthrust tongue without the fingers would be merely rude. Neither gesture is intended to be funny.

Both the boys and the men would use their two fingers to symbolize my body, a body that, without a chink, might seem impenetrable.

The primary meaning of the English word "chink" is a split or crack, a narrow fissure or valley. It derives from the same root as *germ,* as in "germinate." "The connection being in the notion of bursting open," as the Online Etymology Dictionary explains.

Chink also has a racially derogatory meaning, referring to a Chinese person, or, by extension, to any East Asian person, since an English-speaking person using a racially derogatory term would not be expected to differentiate among East Asian peoples.

I have asked boys to differentiate among East Asian peoples. Upon being called a chink, I would say, "You're so stupid! I'm not a chink, I'm a gook!"

The Korean-American comedian Margaret Cho later used a similar statement as a punch line to a joke. I find this joke funny, and some members of a Korean-speaking audience might find this joke funny. I do not know whether other members of an English-speaking audience would find this joke funny.

The term *gook* was used by English-speaking soldiers to refer to Korean people during the Korean War. It was later used by English-speaking soldiers to refer to Vietnamese people during the Vietnam War, since English-speaking soldiers do not differentiate among East Asian people.

The term *gook* may derive from the Korean word for "American"—*miguk.* Hearing Korean people say this word, English-speaking soldiers thought the Korean people were calling themselves gooks ("me gook") and followed suit.

The word *miguk* in Korean means "beautiful country." *Miguk* is a transliteration of the Chinese characters *meiguo,* which also mean "beautiful country."

I know how to pronounce *miguk* but not *meiguo.*

There are several accounts of why *meiguo* came to mean "American." Some claim it's simple phonetic approximation; others claim that *meiguo* was selected out of several possible phonetic approximations by nineteenth-century American missionaries and then made official in the 1901 Boxer Protocol after China's defeat by eight foreign powers. I do not know which account is true.

All commentators seem to agree that neither Korean people nor Chinese people literally believe that America is a beautiful country.

But both Korean people and Chinese people must call America beautiful in order to speak its name.

Neither Korean people nor Chinese people refer to themselves as gooks or chinks.

Neither Korean people nor Chinese people refer to themselves as Korean or Chinese.

Korea is an English word, which seems to derive from a mispronunciation of the name of the Goryeo Dynasty by Silk Road traders that was first recorded by Marco Polo.

China is an English word, which seems to derive from a mispronunciation of the name of the Qin Dynasty by Silk Road traders that was first recorded by Marco Polo.

I have said Marco Polo's name many times in a game that requires you to say his name many times. I do not know the origin of the game. Because of the *r* and the *l,* "Marco Polo" would be a difficult name for Korean speakers to say, but I am not a Korean speaker.

I have called myself a gook many times.

I have called myself a chink only once, when a white high school friend used the term in conversation, then stopped, realizing her gaffe. "Don't worry," I said. "I know what you mean. [X] is such an FOB." "What's an FOB?" she asked. "Fresh off the boat," I said. "I may be a chink, but at least I'm not an FOB." We laughed together, to relieve the tension, although I do not think either of us found my joke funny.

I used the term "FOB" to show that I considered [X] to be foreign, a barbarian. I called myself a chink to make myself seem more American.

Fresh Off the Boat was my white husband's favorite television show during the time we were married. When we watched it, I hoped that laughing at the pushy Chinese immigrant mother on the show would lessen his dislike of my pushy Korean immigrant mother.

I hoped that allowing my white husband to treat my parents as endearingly foreign, fresh off the boat, like the endearingly foreign TV family of *Fresh Off the Boat,* would make me seem more American.

None of the actors in *Fresh Off the Boat* are fresh off the boat. Nearly all of them were born in America. By pretending to be foreign, they make English-speaking audiences feel more American.

My parents are not fresh off the boat. They have been in America for over fifty years. They speak both Korean and English.

A television is a box that allows us to put people inside it.

The television is sometimes called an "idiot box," from the Latin for "private person," from the Greek *idios,* meaning "one's own." But those inside the box have no privacy.

We put the inscrutable into a box so they may be scrutinized.

I made [X] inscrutable. I put [X] into the box.

I made my parents inscrutable. I put my parents into the box.

I decorated the box so it seemed foreign, barbaric. I made the box inscrutable so it seemed like a distant ancestor. I buried it so it seemed like a grave.

I made a chink in the box that the gaze could penetrate.

I stayed outside the box. I treated what was inside the box as a joke.

I was the English-speaking audience.

I watched *Fresh Off the Boat* on the idiot box.

I watched *The Throne* on the idiot box.

In *The Throne* a parent puts his son in the rice chest.

After the son's death, the rice chest is forced open.

After the son's death, his mouth is forced open. Three spoonfuls of rice are forced into his mouth, rice that might have kept him from starving to death in the rice chest.

After the son's death, a name is forced into his mouth.

The name is Sado, a name which has meaning for Korean-speaking audiences.

I have said Sado's name many times.

The son never called himself Sado.

There was never a chink in the rice chest.

No one could see into the rice chest.

There is a "you" in this poem.

You are a member of the English-speaking audience.

I let you see into the box, into what is private, into what is foreign, into what is inscrutable, into what has been buried.

I am the chink in the box.

Frank Paino

The Burning of Giordano Bruno

Rome: 17 February, 1600

> *"Perhaps you, my judges, pronounce this sentence against me with greater fear than I receive it."*
>
> –Giordano Bruno, upon being sentenced to be burned at the stake for heresy

They have driven a spike
through his palate.
As if holding his tongue
might stop the earth in its orbit.

They will set fire to the man
they held seven years
in a lightless cell,
the damp so heavy it numbered
his joints for the counting.

In the marketplace they have
stacked a pyre of sapwood,
green-skinned and rain-moist,
to slow the coming of his
last ragged breath.

The Inquisitors strip him,
chain his arms to the splintered
stake, then step back beneath
embroidered canopies
as the crowd puts torches
to tinder and begins to dance
for god's delight.

Giordano is unafraid.
These hard years have taught him
to drift beyond the shadow
of his flesh, observe the claws
and thumbscrews,
the rakes and studded racks
as if they tore only the body
of an uncanny effigy.

What matter, then, is fire?

He understands their blinkered faith,
their refusal to see
the universe is centered everywhere
without perimeter, and they,
spinning around the planet's
most brilliant star, are kindred
to infinite worlds beyond.

If he could part his lips,
he would proclaim it even now,
as the holy men thrust a silver crucifix
through the shivering wall
of smoke and cinder.

Bruno turns from that dying god
without regret. He has no use
for such brute salvation.
His hair lifts in the updraft,
transforms to fiery wings,
then disappears.
He feels his skin draw closer to bone.

Soon, there will be nothing.

Or, perhaps, something
he could never have supposed.
He gazes down on the gathered

throng: brightly-clothed
women and men—
here and there, a small boy
or girl—a glorious,
dancing host that moves
in tireless orbit around the light
he is becoming.

Yusef Komunyakaa

Facing It

My black face fades,
hiding inside the black granite.
I said I wouldn't,
dammit: No tears.
I'm stone. I'm flesh.
My clouded reflection eyes me
like a bird of prey, the profile of night
slanted against morning. I turn
this way—the stone lets me go.
I turn that way—I'm inside
the Vietnam Veterans Memorial
again, depending on the light
to make a difference.
I go down the 58,022 names,
half-expecting to find
my own in letters like smoke.
I touch the name Andrew Johnson;
I see the booby trap's white flash.
Names shimmer on a woman's blouse
but when she walks away
the names stay on the wall.
Brushstrokes flash, a red bird's
wings cutting across my stare.
The sky. A plane in the sky.
A white vet's image floats
closer to me, then his pale eyes
look through mine. I'm a window.
He's lost his right arm
inside the stone. In the black mirror
a woman's trying to erase names:
No, she's brushing a boy's hair.

Natalie Diaz

Grief Work

Why not now go toward the things I love?

I have walked slow in the garden
of her—: gazed the black flower

dilating her animal-
eye.

I give up my sorrows
the way a bull gives its horns—: astonished,

and wishing there is rest
in the body's softest parts.

Like Jacob's angel, I touched the garnet
of her hip,

and she knew my name,
and I knew hers—:

it was *Auxocromo*, it was *Cromóforo*,
it was *Eliza*.

When the eyes and lips are brushed with honey
what is seen and said will never be the same,

so why not take the apple
in your mouth—:

in flames, in pieces, straight
from the knife's sharp edge?

Achilles chased Hektor around the walls
of Ilium three times—: how long must I circle

the high gate
between her hip and knee

    to solve the red-gold geometry
    of her thigh?

Again the gods put their large hands in me,
move me, break my heart

like a clay jug of wine, loosen a beast
from some darklong depth.

    My melancholy is hoofed.
    I, the terrible beautiful

Lampon, a shining devour-horse tethered
at the bronze manger of her collarbones.

    I do my grief work
    with her body—:

labor to make the emerald tigers
in her throat leap,

lead them burning green to drink
from the deep-violet jetting her breast.

We go where there is love,

to the river, on our knees beneath the sweet
water. I pull her under four times,

    until we are rivered.
    We are rearranged.

I wash the silk and silt of her from my hands—:
now who I come to, I come clean to,

    I come good to.

Danez Smith

alternate names for black boys

1. smoke above the burning bush
2. nemesis of summer night
3. first son of soil
4. coal awaiting spark & wind
5. guilty until proven dead
6. oil heavy starlight
7. monster until proven ghost
8. gone
9. boy
10. phoenix who forgets to un-ash
11. god of shovels & black veils
12. what once passed for kindling
13. fireworks at dawn
14. brilliant, shadow colored coral
15. (I thought to leave this blank
    but who am I to name us nothing?)
16. prayer who learned to bite & sprint
17. a mother's joy & clutched breath

Linda Gregg

Etiology

Cruelty made me. Cruelty and the sweet smelling earth,
and the wet scent of bay. The heave in the rumps
of horses galloping. Heaven forbid that my body not
perish with the rest. I have smelled the rotten wood
after rain and watched maggots writhe on
dead animals. I have lifted the dead owl while it
was still warm. Heaven forbid that I should be saved.

Wisława Szymborska

Psalm

(tr. Stanisław Barańczak and Clare Cavanagh)

Oh, the leaky boundaries of man-made states!
How many clouds float past them with impunity;
how much desert sand shifts from one land to another;
how many mountain pebbles tumble onto foreign soil
in provocative hops!

Need I mention every single bird that flies in the face of frontiers
or alights on the roadblock at the border?
A humble robin—still, its tail resides abroad
while its beak stays home. If that weren't enough, it won't stop bobbing!

Among innumerable insects, I'll single out only the ant
between the border guard's left and right boots
blithely ignoring the questions "Where from?" and "Where to?"

Oh, to register in detail, at a glance, the chaos
prevailing on every continent!
Isn't that a privet on the far bank
smuggling its hundred-thousandth leaf across the river?
And who but the octopus, with impudent long arms,
would disrupt the sacred bounds of territorial waters?

And how can we talk of order overall
when the very placement of the stars
leaves us doubting just what shines for whom?

Not to speak of the fog's reprehensible drifting!
And dust blowing all over the steppes
as if they hadn't been partitioned!
And the voices coasting on obliging airwaves,
that conspiratorial squeaking, those indecipherable mutters!

Only what is human can truly be foreign.
The rest is mixed vegetation, subversive moles, and wind.

Kaveh Akbar

Orchids Are Sprouting from the Floorboards

Orchids are sprouting from the floorboards.
Orchids are gushing out from the faucets.
The cat mews orchids from his mouth.
His whiskers are also orchids.
The grass is sprouting orchids.
It is becoming mostly orchids.
The trees are filled with orchids.
The tire swing is twirling with orchids.
The sunlight on the wet cement is a white orchid.
The car's tires leave a trail of orchids.
A bouquet of orchids lifts from its tailpipe.
Teenagers are texting each other pictures
of orchids on their phones, which are also orchids.
Old men in orchid penny loafers
furiously trade orchids.
Mothers fill bottles with warm orchids
to feed their infants, who are orchids themselves.
Their coos are a kind of orchid.
The clouds are all orchids.
They are raining orchids.
The walls are all orchids,
the teapot is an orchid,
the blank easel is an orchid,
and this cold is an orchid. Oh,
Lydia, we miss you terribly.

Tracy K. Smith

Wade in the Water

for the Geechee Gullah Ring Shouters

One of the women greeted me.
I love you, she said. She didn't
Know me, but I believed her,
And a terrible new ache
Rolled over in my chest,
Like in a room where the drapes
Have been swept back. I love you,
I love you, as she continued
Down the hall past other strangers,
Each feeling pierced suddenly
By pillars of heavy light.
I love you, throughout
The performance, in every
Handclap, every stomp.
I love you in the rusted iron
Chains someone was made
To drag until love let them be
Unclasped and left empty
In the center of the ring.
I love you in the water
Where they pretended to wade,
Singing that old blood-deep song
That dragged us to those banks
And cast us in. I love you,
The angles of it scraping at
Each throat, shouldering past
The swirling dust motes
In those beams of light
That whatever we now knew
We could let ourselves feel, knew

To climb. O Woods—O Dogs—
O Tree—O Gun—*O Girl, run*—
O Miraculous Many Gone—
O Lord—O Lord—O Lord—
Is this love the trouble you promised?

Ocean Vuong

Telemachus

Like any good son, I pull my father out
of the water, drag him by his hair

through white sand, his knuckles carving a trail
the waves rush in to erase. Because the city

beyond the shore is no longer
where we left it. Because the bombed

cathedral is now a cathedral
of trees. I kneel beside him to see how far

I might sink. *Do you know who I am,*
Ba? But the answer never comes. The answer

is the bullet hole in his back, brimming
with seawater. He is so still I think

he could be anyone's father, found
the way a green bottle might appear

at a boy's feet containing a year
he has never touched. I touch

his ears. No use. I turn him
over. To face it. The cathedral

in his sea-black eyes. The face
not mine—but one I will wear

to kiss all my lovers good-night:
the way I seal my father's lips

with my own & begin
the faithful work of drowning.

Aracelis Girmay

Kingdom Animalia

When I get the call about my brother,
I'm on a stopped train leaving town
& the news packs into me—freight—
though it's him on the other end
now, saying *finefine*—

Forfeit my eyes, I want to turn away
from the hair on the floor of his house
& how it got there Monday,
but my one heart falls
like a sad, fat persimmon
dropped by the hand of the Turczyn's old tree.

I want to sleep. I do not want to sleep. See,

one day, not today, not now, we will be gone
from this earth where we know the gladiolas.
My brother, this noise,
some love [you] I loved
with all my brain, & breath,
will be gone; I've been told, today, to consider this
as I ride the long tracks out & dream so good

I see a plant in the window of the house
my brother shares with his love, their shoes. & there
he is, asleep in bed
with this same woman whose long skin
covers all of her bones, in a city called Oakland,
& their dreams hang above them
a little like a chandelier, & their teeth
flash in the night, oh, body.

Oh, body, be held now by whom you love.
Whole years will be spent, underneath these impossible stars,
when dirt's the only animal who will sleep with you
& touch you with
its mouth.

Carl Phillips

In a Low Voice, Slowly

So stubborn, and as if almost necessary, this
        little wind, playing the leaves, their surfaces, playing
the leaves where they lie fallen, while not once
        rearranging them. Like being asked what, if anything,
do you regret at this point; and, as answer, shaping
        your own smallish song around how knowing isn't
understanding, isn't mystery either, which isn't *un*-knowing,
        not exactly, more like deciding to turn abruptly
east after so many years westering, what kind of answer
        was that? Sometimes the past seems the stuff of heraldry,
figures proper on a ground of good and evil. Other times
        the past sways ocean-like above me. There's a sound
deer still make when in sixes they come down
        from the hills at sunrise, the kind of sunrise where
no sun's visible, but it's daylight, and just the rain, and
        the deer passing like their own form of light through it;
their hooves mark the damp ground incidentally,
        no particular meaning. It's true that love marks the body.

Diane Seuss

High Romance

And then Keats's ghost found
that he could no longer love
Fanny Brawne. He'd escaped
the body like a love
letter from its envelope, and he'd flown
like a love letter in a windstorm.
He'd seen that the words
formed from ink melted in the rain.
Words, he now knew—and he'd once been
such a devotee—didn't matter,
or didn't matter so much as he'd believed
they mattered. Something mattered, he knew,
but whatever it was he couldn't put
words to it, or he didn't have the heart
to put words to it. He did feel love,
but it was an arrow without a target.
It was diffuse, like an atomized
perfume, or stars as the poor see them,
who cannot afford glasses. He saw
that Fanny, as she was known,
was a concept, just as he had been a concept.
They each inhabited the same amount
of space, like a tablespoon
of butter and a tablespoon of lard.
In a book, they would each occupy
a single page. Their brains, encased
in cranial bones and flesh and heads of hair,
could each rest on a single silk pillow.
Ideas, he found, don't die. Even notions fly
like cottonwood seeds through the air.
And love had been a notion. He saw
that Fanny, in time, would slip free of herself—
everything does, in time, even roses,
even stones, foothills, fleas, and poems.

Rhyme, he saw, existed on its own behalf.
He could catch it like a bird catches
an air current. From above, he could see
that Fanny was not trifling. Nothing,
from above, is trifling, nor more compelling
than anything else. His love for her, he saw,
had been an invention of the mind.
Only belief could sustain it, but he
could no longer sustain belief. Now
and then he'd try it on again—love—
like a fancy hat he could not afford
and now appeared ludicrously overdesigned.
Once, his ghost managed to look at her again,
through the gauzy curtains that hung
over her bedroom window. His gaze
was too objective to find her beautiful,
but objectivity itself—that was beautiful.

Nathan McClain

The Ferry

I still had a lover. Maybe let's start there.
I hitched a ride to Boston, where I missed
the ferry by what seemed like minutes. But time
can work that way in the mind. I was in love
or wanted to be in love and there was distance
everywhere is maybe a better way to put it,
though what exactly was *it*, I hadn't given it
a designation. I looked for the boat, it wasn't there:
only the dock, a few seagulls, a blue distance.
If I was supposed to wave goodbye, I missed
my chance, though what did I care, so in love
with solitude, at least I was at the time.
It seemed easy, being lonely, watching time
lapse, that boat long dispatched, I'd missed it
yet there I was waving, like a fool in love
perhaps, at what? I couldn't tell. I wasn't there
when the ferry left, remember, I missed
it, or they went on without me. The distance
made it hard to see clearly where distance
ended, or if it did. Or I didn't make it in time
to see, maybe time was against me. I missed
the ferry, I had no money. The ferryman said *It*
was fine and smiled at me. Smiled. There
was the shore and me wanting to be in love
though I wasn't. I carried what I could. Love?
I didn't have room for it. In the distance,
I swore my solitude waved. I missed it where
I was headed, sure, but there was hardly time
for that. The boat was early. I boarded it
and stood on the stern. Part of me was missing,
but there had to be a cost. That part I missed—
my mind a rough sea I might have loved
watching lap were I not so inside it—
my mind the fish, too, the shore distant

as the voice I thought I heard in it, as time
itself. The ferry was late. I was there
hoping I missed it. I didn't trust the distance,
lovely as it seemed. I didn't trust time
nor where it carried me. I knew what was there.

francine j. harris

enough food and a mom

The dad. body has just enough gravy on his plate to sop up one piece of bread.
So, enough for one supper, says the mom. She comes back to him, says
don't argue with mom, you're a ghost. There's enough water around to drown a cob
in its husk. in a dad. He puts up weather stripping all night. to keep out the mom. He says

I should have cooked for you more. She thinks she could make her own insulin.
to keep from going into dad.

She says I should have married a ghost. says: You have a little
raisin on your lip. a little. The mom says stop all that quiet, it's foolish. Come on
now, dad. come to ghost. says the ghost.

I won't even warn the mom. I won't even flinch if the ghost tries to hold her mom. After all,
a good séance starts with enough food and a mom. The ghost with a biscuit in meat. The
mom with the smell of cracked dad. sucked out of oxygen. The mom is
a smell of wrecked vines.

You, the dad. with no teeth. And no, (the mom)
is a garden full of ghost. No. says the dad: lost in ashes.

No city is complete. its own worst ghost. who can't remember the ghost
now, the ghost says: All your selves know, now. They ghost
like the bushel of a snowflower.

Everyone is dead. now. says, the ghost. The mom is a yard of blackening petals.

At night, I have really long dads. Without the ghosts, I wake in a puddle of ghost.
But you'll be mom one day. to know I am alive. We are all sappy dad, aren't
we. Tell the ghost, it's ok. Let the bodies lie ghost for a while.

I mom of you. I mom of you a lot.

Wendy Cope

To My Husband

If we were never going to die, I might
Not hug you quite as often or as tight,
Or say goodbye to you as carefully
If I were certain you'd come back to me.
Perhaps I wouldn't value every day,
Every act of kindness, every laugh

As much, if I knew you and I could stay
For ever as each other's other half.
We may not have too many years before
One disappears to the eternal yonder
And I can't hug or touch you any more.
Yes, of course that knowledge makes us fonder.
Would I want to change things, if I could,

And make us both immortal? Love, I would.

Agha Shahid Ali

Farewell

At a certain point I lost track of you.
They make a desolation and call it peace.
when you left even the stones were buried:
the defenseless would have no weapons.

When the ibex rubs itself against the rocks,
who collects its fallen fleece from the slopes?
O Weaver whose seams perfectly vanished,
who weighs the hairs on the jeweler's balance?
They make a desolation and call it peace.
Who is the guardian tonight of the Gates of Paradise?

My memory is again in the way of your history.
Army convoys all night like desert caravans:
In the smoking oil of dimmed headlights, time dissolved—all winter—its crushed fennel.
We can't ask them: Are you done with the world?

In the lake the arms of temples and mosques are locked in each other's reflections.

Have you soaked saffron to pour on them when they are found like this
centuries later in this country
I have stitched to your shadow?

In this country we step out with doors in our arms
Children run out with windows in their arms.
You drag it behind you in lit corridors.
If the switch is pulled you will be torn from everything.

At a certain point I lost track of you.
You needed me. You needed to perfect me.
In your absence you polished me into the Enemy.
Your history gets in the way of my memory.
I am everything you lost. You can't forgive me.

I am everything you lost. Your perfect Enemy.
Your memory gets in the way of my memory:

I am being rowed through Paradise in a river of Hell:
Exquisite ghost, it is night.

The paddle is a heart; it breaks the porcelain waves.
It is still night. The paddle is a lotus.
I am rowed—as it withers—toward the breeze which is soft as
if it had pity on me.

If only somehow you could have been mine, what wouldn't
have happened in the world?

I'm everything you lost. You won't forgive me.
My memory keeps getting in the way of your history.
There is nothing to forgive. You can't forgive me.
I hid my pain even from myself; I revealed my pain only to myself.

There is everything to forgive. You can't forgive me.

If only somehow you could have been mine,
what would not have been possible in the world?

Adam Zagajewski

Try to Praise the Mutilated World

(tr. Clare Cavanagh)

Try to praise the mutilated world.
Remember June's long days,
and wild strawberries, drops of rosé wine.
The nettles that methodically overgrow
the abandoned homesteads of exiles.
You must praise the mutilated world.
You watched the stylish yachts and ships;
one of them had a long trip ahead of it,
while salty oblivion awaited others.
You've seen the refugees going nowhere,
you've heard the executioners sing joyfully.
You should praise the mutilated world.
Remember the moments when we were together
in a white room and the curtain fluttered.
Return in thought to the concert where music flared.
You gathered acorns in the park in autumn
and leaves eddied over the earth's scars.
Praise the mutilated world
and the gray feather a thrush lost,
and the gentle light that strays and vanishes
and returns.

Morgan Parker

Search for the New Land

The future is not a gender, doesn't even have a body.
And then there's white women
making T-shirts and selling them for eighty dollars or whatever.
Whatever they do.
The sun doesn't hate anyone and neither do I.
All I listen to is Lee Morgan's trumpet
for long stretches of afternoons and nights in the desert.
I decide on the delusion where I live,
genderless and out of sight. This is how I choose
to spend what I have. I'm an American,
so I hear only what I want to.
This is our right—
to protect ourselves in times of extreme stress.
In times of great fear,
we do what we have to do to survive.
Our task is to make it out alive.
This one instruction for having a body,
the punishment for it.
I see the way birds look at me—
Endangered. The future is only earned
or inherited. It writes itself.
Everything wrong with the picture
is the true meaning of the picture.
The future is relative—of course
I am conditional. I am writing this from the deep end.
There are some privileges to being feared,
fearing the consequences of yourself.
How I came all this way and all these centuries,
carrying this extreme stress and pervading American fear.
The taxi driver deposited my many suitcases
into the busy street and drove off.
I don't have enough hands. My evolution
has not equipped me for this climate.
Lifting a box of books into the overhead compartment,

I wished for a device to make my face a white girl
in times like these, helpless with a body. No full flight
would watch a white girl struggle this way,
her life flashing before her
under the weight of her own books.
I can't even imagine it. The dissonance of chords
and notes, the hilarious idea of infinity.
The last time I considered suicide—on the edge
of a curb, leaning into the yellow taxis of
the Meatpacking, which in retrospect would have been
a terrible place to die, in front of all those white women
hobbling in their high heels over the cobblestone,
doing that shampoo commercial move,
bathed in the light of themselves—I considered
all I've learned about sacrifice, and duty.
I went home in an American SUV, ashamed of something.
That last time I teased death, I couldn't
listen to any music for weeks, not one note of song.
When I think of the story of Abraham
tying up his son for slaughter—the offering
on an altar at the edge of a mountaintop,
the instruction to do what he had to do, as it is written—
I identify most with the ram. The alternative
asymmetrical sacrifice. I see the way
birds look at me—it writes itself.
We used to sing that song, *Father Abraham*
had many sons, I am one of them
and so are you, praising the lord and fearing
the wind in our palm trees. The future is this awe:
looking up at the sky in California. Blue in Green.
I am always at the edge of the end of the world.
In the desert, if a ram appears, I may escape death.
Eighty dollars for a certain and secure future.
Miles Davis's trumpet on "Blue in Green"—a future
where I no longer need to be grateful.
Baldwin wrote, "Our crown has already been bought
and paid for." What's important in these times of
war and faith is the consideration, the lean into traffic,

the ax raised dutifully. You are always almost gone—
it is written so that we may remember.
Documentation of the past makes the future possible.
I am learning all I can from this day so I can teach it
to who I will be tomorrow. I have written
I am a different person every minute, and everybody knows
I don't believe in time, anyway. I did not inherit it.
I always misremember the title *Search for the New Land*,
the Lee Morgan album and the book by Julius Lester.
I misremember the THE. I think: a new land.
A—all I can hear is *go*. Wherever, anywhere but here.
In Julius Lester's *Search for the New Land*, it is written,
"Being. To be. In America one was taught TO DO."
My task is to wander until I find a safe place
to continue being. I think: effort, and sacrifice,
and faith—fingers crossed.
I think: it is my responsibility to find
the ram to slaughter in my place.
If we hate the past more than we love the future,
Julius Lester wrote, *we will succeed in bringing that past*
into the future. Documentation of the past
makes all futures possible, makes the Land New.
The the: it is written. The difference between surviving
and Being. The future is—
take it. The future is out of body,
out of sight, certain as the the.
Looking up at the sky in California.
The trumpet again and again—
wind, blue, one holy bird and everything
possible and promised. The New Land
already waiting for me. Even me.

Osip Mandelstam

And I Was Alive

(tr. Christian Wiman)

And I was alive in the blizzard of the blossoming pear,
Myself I stood in the storm of the bird-cherry tree.
It was all leaflife and starshower, unerring, self-shattering power,
And it was all aimed at me.

What is this dire delight flowering fleeing always earth?
What is being? What is truth?

Blossoms rupture and rapture the air,
All hover and hammer,
Time intensified and time intolerable, sweetness raveling rot.
It is now. It is not.

(May 4, 1937)

Anne Carson

O Small Sad Ecstasy of Love

I like being with you all night with closed eyes.
What luck—here you are
coming
along the stars!
I did a road trip
all over my mind and heart
and
there you were
kneeling by the roadside
with your little toolkit
fixing something.

Give me a world, you have taken the world I was.

James Wright

Lying in a Hammock at William Duffy's Farm in Pine Island, Minnesota

Over my head, I see the bronze butterfly,
Asleep on the black trunk,
Blowing like a leaf in green shadow.
Down the ravine behind the empty house,
The cowbells follow one another
Into the distances of the afternoon.
To my right,
In a field of sunlight between two pines,
The droppings of last year's horses
Blaze up into golden stones.
I lean back, as the evening darkens and comes on.
A chicken hawk floats over, looking for home.
I have wasted my life.

Christian Wiman

Love's Last

Love's last urgency is earth
and grief is all gravity

and the long fall always
back to earliest hours

that exist nowhere
but in one's brain.

From the hard-packed
pile of old-mown grass,

from boredom, from pain,
a boy's random slash

unlocks a dark ardor
of angry bees

that link the trees
and block his way home.

I like to hold him holding me,
mystery mastering fear,

so young, standing unstung
under what survives of sky.

I learned too late how to live.
Child, teach me how to die.

Jericho Brown

Duplex

A poem is a gesture toward home.
It makes dark demands I call my own.

    Memory makes demands darker than my own:
    My last love drove a burgundy car.

My first love drove a burgundy car.
He was fast and awful, tall as my father.

    Steadfast and awful, my tall father
    Hit hard as a hailstorm. He'd leave marks.

Light rain hits easy but leaves its own mark
Like the sound of a mother weeping again.

    Like the sound of my mother weeping again,
    No sound beating ends where it began.

None of the beaten end up how we began.
A poem is a gesture toward home.

Nicole Sealey

Object Permanence

for John

We wake as if surprised the other is still there,
each petting the sheet to be sure.

How have we managed our way
to this bed—beholden to heat like dawn

indebted to light. Though we're not so self-
important as to think everything

has led to this, everything has led to this.
There's a name for the animal

love makes of us—named, I think,
like rain, for the sound it makes.

You are the animal after whom other animals
are named. Until there's none left to laugh,

days will start with the same startle
and end with caterpillars gorged on milkweed.

O, how we entertain the angels
with our brief animation. O,

how I'll miss you when we're dead.

Morri Creech

Provision

Nothing we tried could coax sweetness
from my grandfather's apple tree.
Year after year we tended the branches,
propped the broken boughs with scraps of lumber.
Year after year those hunched limbs
dragged the ground and bore a withered fruit
nothing could eat, not even the neighbor's horses.
So who cared when, one winter, lightning
tore a smoldering seam down its trunk?
My grandfather left the tree alone all season,
figuring the rain-soaked husk not fit for burning.

That April, axes in hand, we crossed the field
to clear the warped remains. My grandfather
leaned down and stuck his hand inside
the storm-struck hollow, as though
to touch blighted heartwood.
He jerked his hand back, cursing, wringing fire
from his palm—and as we ran toward the house
the whole tree seemed to come alive at once,
swarming and quickening with bees
that had settled there to make honey in the wound.

Paige Lewis

You Can Take Off Your Sweater, I've Made Today Warm

Sit on the park bench and chew this mint leaf.
Right now, way above your head, two men

floating in a rocket ship are ignoring their
delicate experiments, their buttons flashing

red. Watching you chew your mint, the men
forget about their gritty toothpaste, about

their fingers, numb from lack of gravity.
They see you and, for the first time since

liftoff, think *home*. When they were boys
they were gentle. And smart. One could

tie string around a fly without cinching it
in half. One wrote tales of sailors who

drowned after mistaking the backs of
whales for islands. Does it matter which

man is which? They just quit their mission
for you. They're on their way down. You'll

take both men—a winter husband and
a summer husband. Does it matter which

is—don't slump like that. Get up, we have
so much work to do before—   wait   you're going

the wrong   way   small whelp of a woman!   this is not

        how we   behave   where are you going

this world is already   willing

to give you anything   do you want to know Latin

okay   now everyone

here knows Latin   want inflatable   deer
deer !   i promise the winter /

summer children will barely hurt   dear   i'm hurt
that you would ever think

i don't glisten to you   i'm always glistening

tame your voice   and   turn around

the men are coming   they've traded everything for you
the gemmy   starlight

the click   click   click

of the universe expanding

stop

aren't you known   aren't you
known here

how can you be certain that anywhere else will provide

more pears than you could ever eat

remember the sweet rot of it all

come back   you forgot your sweater

what if there's nothing there when you—

you don't have your

sweater

what if it's cold

Ross Gay

Catalog of Unabashed Gratitude

Friends, will you bear with me today,
for I have awakened
from a dream in which a robin
made with its shabby wings a kind of veil
behind which it shimmied and stomped something from the south
of Spain, its breast aflare,
looking me dead in the eye
from the branch that grew into my window,
coochie-cooing my chin,
the bird shuffling its little talons left, then right,
while the leaves bristled
against the plaster wall, two of them drifting
onto my blanket while the bird
opened and closed its wings like a matador
giving up on murder,
jutting its beak, turning a circle,
and flashing, again,
the ruddy bombast of its breast
by which I knew upon waking
it was telling me
in no uncertain terms
to bellow forth the tubas and sousaphones,
the whole rusty brass band of gratitude
not quite dormant in my belly—
it said so in a human voice,
"Bellow forth"—
and who among us could ignore such odd
and precise counsel?

Hear ye! hear ye! I am here
to holler that I have hauled tons—by which I don't mean lots,
I mean *tons*—of cow shit
and stood ankle deep in swales of maggots
swirling the spent beer grains

the brewery man was good enough to dump off
holding his nose, for they smell very bad,
but make the compost writhe giddy and lick its lips,
twirling dung with my pitchfork
again and again
with hundreds and hundreds of other people,
we dreamt an orchard this way,
furrowing our brows,
and hauling our wheelbarrows,
and sweating through our shirts,
and less than a year later there was a party
at which trees were sunk into the well-fed earth,
one of which, a liberty apple, after being watered in
was tamped by a baby barefoot
with a bow hanging in her hair
biting her lip in her joyous work
and friends this is the realest place I know,
it makes me squirm like a worm I am so grateful,
you could ride your bike there
or roller skate or catch the bus
there is a fence and a gate twisted by hand,
there is a fig tree taller than you in Indiana,
it will make you gasp.
It might make you want to stay alive even, thank you;

and thank you
for not taking my pal when the engine
of his mind dragged him
to swig fistfuls of Xanax and a bottle or two of booze,
and thank you for taking my father
a few years after his own father went down thank you
mercy, mercy, thank you
for not smoking meth with your mother
oh thank you thank you
for leaving and for coming back,
and thank you for what inside my friends'
love bursts like a throng of roadside goldenrod

gleaming into the world,
likely hauling a shovel with her
like one named Aralee ought,
with hands big as a horse's,
and who, like one named Aralee ought,
will laugh time to time til the juice
runs from her nose; oh
thank you
for the way a small thing's wail makes
the milk or what once was milk
in us gather into horses
huckle-buckling across a field;

and thank you, friends, when last spring
the hyacinth bells rang
and the crocuses flaunted
their upturned skirts, and a quiet roved
the beehive which when I entered
were snugged two or three dead
fist-sized clutches of bees between the frames,
almost clinging to one another,
this one's tiny head pushed
into another's tiny wing,
one's forelegs resting on another's face,
the translucent paper of their wings fluttering
beneath my breath and when
a few dropped to the frames beneath:
honey; and after falling down to cry,
everything's glacial shine.

And thank *you*, too. And thanks
for the corduroy couch I have put you on.
Put your feet up. Here's a light blanket,
a pillow, dear one,
for I think this is going to be long.
I can't stop
my gratitude, which includes, dear reader,

you, for staying here with me,
for moving your lips just so as I speak.
Here is a cup of tea. I have spooned honey into it.

And thank you the tiny bee's shadow
perusing these words as I write them.
And the way my love talks quietly
when in the hive,
so quietly, in fact, you cannot hear her
but only notice barely her lips moving
in conversation. Thank you what does not scare her
in me, but makes her reach my way. Thank you the love
she is which hurts sometimes. And the time
she misremembered elephants
in one of my poems which, oh, here
they come, garlanded with morning glory and wisteria
blooms, trombones all the way down to the river.
Thank you the quiet
in which the river bends around the elephant's
solemn trunk, polishing stones, floating
on its gentle back
the flock of geese flying overhead.

And to the quick and gentle flocking
of men to the old lady falling down
on the corner of Fairmount and 18th, holding patiently
with the softest parts of their hands
her cane and purple hat,
gathering for her the contents of her purse
and touching her shoulder and elbow;
thank you the cockeyed court
on which in a half-court 3 vs. 3 we oldheads
made of some runny-nosed kids
a shambles, and the 61-year-old
after flipping a reverse layup off a back door cut
from my no-look pass to seal the game
ripped off his shirt and threw punches at the gods
and hollered at the kids to admire the pacemaker's scar

grinning across his chest; thank you
the glad accordion's wheeze
in the chest; thank you the bagpipes.

Thank you to the woman barefoot in a gaudy dress
for stopping her car in the middle of the road
and the tractor trailer behind her, and the van behind it,
whisking a turtle off the road.
Thank you god of gaudy.
Thank you paisley panties.
Thank you the organ up my dress.
Thank you the sheer dress you wore kneeling in my dream
at the creek's edge and the light
swimming through it. The koi kissing
halos into the glassy air.
The room in my mind with the blinds drawn
where we nearly injure each other
crawling into the shawl of the other's body.
Thank you for saying it plain:
fuck each other dumb.

And you, again, you, for the true kindness
it has been for you to remain awake
with me like this, nodding time to time
and making that noise which I take to mean
yes, or, *I understand*, or, *please go on*
but not too long, or, *why are you spitting*
so much, or, *easy Tiger*
hands to yourself. I am excitable.
I am sorry. I am grateful.
I just want us to be friends now, forever.
Take this bowl of blackberries from the garden.
The sun has made them warm.
I picked them just for you. I promise
I will try to stay on my side of the couch.

And thank you the baggie of dreadlocks I found in a drawer
while washing and folding the clothes of our murdered friend;

the photo in which his arm slung
around the sign to "the trail of silences"; thank you
the way before he died he held
his hands open to us; for coming back
in a waft of incense or in the shape of a boy
in another city looking
from between his mother's legs,
or disappearing into the stacks after brushing by;
for moseying back in dreams where,
seeing us lost and scared
he put his hand on our shoulders
and pointed us to the temple across town;

and thank you to the man all night long
hosing a mist on his early-bloomed
peach tree so that the hard frost
not waste the crop, the ice
in his beard and the ghosts
lifting from him when the warming sun
told him *sleep now*; thank you
the ancestor who loved you
before she knew you
by smuggling seeds into her braid for the long
journey, who loved you
before he knew you by putting
a walnut tree in the ground, who loved you
before she knew you by not slaughtering
the land; thank you
who did not bulldoze the ancient grove
of dates and olives,
who sailed his keys into the ocean
and walked softly home; who did not fire, who did not
plunge the head into the toilet, who said *stop,*
don't do that; who lifted some broken
someone up; who volunteered
the way a plant birthed of the reseeding plant
is called a *volunteer*, like the plum tree

that marched beside the raised bed
in my garden, like the arugula that marched
itself between the blueberries,
nary a bayonet, nary an army, nary a nation,
which usage of the word volunteer
familiar to gardeners the wide world
made my pal shout "Oh!" and dance
and plunge his knuckles
into the lush soil before gobbling two strawberries
and digging a song from his guitar
made of wood from a tree someone planted, thank you;

thank you zinnia, and gooseberry, rudbeckia
and pawpaw, Ashmead's kernel, cockscomb
and scarlet runner, feverfew and lemonbalm;
thank you knitbone and sweetgrass and sunchoke
and false indigo whose petals stammered apart
by bumblebees good lord please give me a minute...
and moonglow and catkin and crookneck
and painted tongue and seedpod and johnny jump-up;
thank you what in us rackets glad
what gladrackets us;

and thank you, too, this knuckleheaded heart, this pelican heart,
this gap-toothed heart flinging open its gaudy maw
to the sky, oh clumsy, oh bumblefucked,
oh giddy, oh dumbstruck,
oh rickshaw, oh goat twisting
its head at me from my peach tree's highest branch,
balanced impossibly gobbling the last fruit,
its tongue working like an engine,
a lone sweet drop tumbling by some miracle
into my mouth like the smell of someone I've loved;
heart like an elephant screaming
at the bones of its dead;
heart like the lady on the bus
dressed head to toe in gold, the sun

shivering her shiny boots, singing
Erykah Badu to herself
leaning her head against the window;

and thank you the way my father one time came back in a dream
by plucking the two cables beneath my chin
like a bass fiddle's strings
and played me until I woke singing,
no kidding, singing, smiling,
thank you, thank you,
stumbling into the garden where
the Juneberry's flowers had burst open
like the bells of French horns, the lily
my mother and I planted oozed into the air,
the bazillion ants labored in their earthen workshops
below, the collard greens waved in the wind
like the sails of ships, and the wasps
swam in the mint bloom's viscous swill;

and you, again you, for hanging tight, dear friend.
I know I can be long-winded sometimes.
I want so badly to rub the sponge of gratitude
over every last thing, including you, which, yes, awkward,
the suds in your ear and armpit, the little sparkling gems
slipping into your eye. Soon it will be over,

which is precisely what the child in my dream said,
holding my hand, pointing at the roiling sea and the sky
hurtling our way like so many buffalo,
who said *it's much worse than we think,*
and sooner, to whom I said
no duh child in my dreams, what do you think
this singing and shuddering is,
what this screaming and reaching and dancing
and crying is, other than loving
what every second goes away?
Goodbye, I mean to say.
And thank you. Every day.

Leonard Cohen

When I Left the King

When I left the king I began to rehearse what I would say to the world: long rehearsals full of revisions, imaginary applause, humiliations, edicts of revenge. I grew swollen as I conspired with my ambition, I struggled, I expanded, and when the term was up, I gave birth to an ape. After some small inevitable misunderstanding, the ape turned on me. Limping, stumbling, I fled back to the swept courtyards of the king. "Where is your ape?" the king demanded. "Bring me your ape." The work is slow. The ape is old. He clowns behind his bars, imitating our hands in the dream. He winks at my official sense of urgency. What king? he wants to know. What courtyard? What highway?

Jorie Graham

Mother and Child (The Road at the Edge of the Field)

The grasses midsummer eve when the stems grow invisible and the
seemingly de-
capitated heads like a flock
that is not in the end departing but is lingering, golden with
buttery flies then also aglow with
orange—gnats
hovering their tiny solar system round—heads
bending this way and that in
unison glowing and not
showing where they
are attached to earth or what path has brought them to their
status; they for whom stasis
when it comes is the huge
inholding of breath by the whole
world as it is seen to be here, horizon to horizon stilling,
down to this corner field of grasses
held, bees all molten
with approach and with-
drawal—though of course there are still stars—albeit now in-
visible—and I look up into the
sky to see
beyond the foaming of
day's end the place where all in fact
is, longed-for or over-
looked altogether by the mind,
human, which can,
if it wishes,
ken them into view
by imagination—there is no invention—or not—as long as it
exists, the mind can
do this—
how many are the years you have
say the grass-pointings
which if I follow them up

and up
make of my eyeing large spidery webtrails into
the galaxy thank
god, and all that outlives
for sure the me in
me—a whirling robe humming with firstness greets you if you eye-up, confess it—
in letters home you would
tell this whole story but
nothing happened—the world opened its robe
and you
were free to look with
no sense of
excitement, no song, it is so simple, your lungs afloat, your
shears still there in your right
hand, the hedgerow wild beside you and how you can—yes—hear it
course up through its million
stalks—and also, closely
now, the single
skinny stalk—and how it is
true, all *is* being sucked up by the soil into the sky, and the sky
back down into variegation and
forking and fingery
elaboration at the core of prior
elaboration—spotted, in-
candescent—each about to be cast off by the one coming
behind—it too shall
contribute
to the
possible—the world of the world—and the shears
in my right hand grow warm
with the sun they've been hanging in, and I talk to myself, I make
words that follow from other
words, they push from be-
hind—into the hedge like the
hedge but not of it—no—not
ever—slippery against it where it
never knows they are pressing, delirious accents trying to reach in, fit
in—phantoms—as the calls

of the disappeared in the stadiums today are in-
audible, the satellite's announcement
of capture inaudible, the occupation of an
other's body, taken from its
private life its bed its
window its still half-open
fridge, dragged down the stairs with everyone
screaming—have you visited your
loved ones
recently says the guard as he lets loose the filamentary
shock of electricity through the body to the
heart whose words
will now
cease—what is cruelty—the grasses lean
all one way now under the sway of
difference, which evening's drop of
temperature brings on,
which the guard and the prisoner feel as one,
grassheads like spume on the thin shanks
of stalk—their until-now right there
beneath them—*grass*, I say,
grass, and rip a piece to hold out to you
who stand beneath me not yet speaking—everyone awaits
your first word—and I open your hand
and put the heads inside it and close it and I watch
terror spray from you in
colonies of tiny glances—everywhere but where
your hand is, and then
stalk I say, *poppy*, *thorn*, *hedgerose*—I am
not screaming because I am
old enough to hang on hang on
but your small heart beating as of two years now hears the
cannibalizing crossed scream in all
my kindness—the mother
stands beside you and she sees you stare at her and put
your arm down and open your
fist and we both see the seeds drop

down onto the asphalt and the ground-breeze drag them
a little distance
to the middle
of the road
then stop. It is summer. It is the solstice. A diamond of energy
holds us. We breathe, and
what we call
the next moment between us,
where I take your empty hand and
we start home,
emptied of attempt and emptied of
survival skill,
is *love.*

Keith Flynn

The Glory Façade

No one gets the life they deserve.

Eternity is not the endless passage
of time, uninterrupted.
It is contained in a single moment,
where time has stopped,
a frozen moat,
a conversation with a stone.

Each year a column, slowly tilting.
"God is the only architect,"
sd. Gaudí. "I merely copy."
He became a studious imitator
of the tree, the river, the wind.

Light builds everything,
strings of light
torn from sheer blocks,
streamers inviting you
to reconnect them;
the tails of comets,
the rocket's smoky trail
mixed among vaporous clouds,
mist off a boiling pot,
the searching vine's restless rivulets.

Gaudí was killed by a streetcar,
seditiously moored to its tracks,
unable to pass through him,
or follow his immense light.

Buildings are made of music,
rising with purpose,
filling the air's geometry with forms.
Cities should be built
from the worship
of nothing in
particular,
and filled with the feelings
of its people, the only mortar
that can reinforce the beams.

From this I make my life a bell
and hurl its chime
across the expanse,
and a gong of years develops,
buttressed by nothing.

The spool of that life
is filled with temporary commotions,
knowing that a human being
in love with mystery
is never finished

Acknowledgments

The editors are grateful to Elizabeth Scanlon at *American Poetry Review* for originally publishing our introductory essay/conversation, "Aesthetics and Ethics in Poetic Closure."

This project benefited greatly from research assistance by Elisabeth Beck, Monika Cassel, and Holly Marie Moore, as well as administrative assistance from Lila Rutishauser. Thank you!

Permissions

"Orchids Are Sprouting from the Floorboards" from *Calling a Wolf a Wolf*. Copyright © 2017 by Kaveh Akbar. Reprinted by permission of The Permissions Company, LLC on behalf of Alice James Books (www.alicejamesbooks.org) and by permission of Penguin Books, Ltd.

"My Faith Gets Grime Under Its Nails" from *Theophanies*. Copyright © 2024 by Sarah Ghazal Ali. Reprinted by permission of The Permissions Company, LLC on behalf of Alice James Books, www.alicejamesbooks.org.

"Farewell" from *The Country Without a Post Office*. Copyright © 1997 by Agha Shahid Ali. Reprinted by permission of W. W. Norton & Company, Inc.

"The Way" from *Veil: New and Selected Poems*. Copyright © 2001 by Rae Armantrout. Reprinted by permission of Wesleyan University Press.

"Meditations in an Emergency" from *Dispatch*. Copyright © 2019 by Cameron Awkward-Rich. Reprinted by permission of Persea Books, Inc, www.perseabooks.com. All rights reserved.

"Relax" from *Like a Beggar*. Copyright © 2014 by Ellen Bass. Reprinted by permission of The Permissions Company, LLC on behalf of Copper Canyon Press, www.coppercanyonpress.org.

"Duplex [A poem is a gesture toward home]" from *The Tradition*. Copyright © 2019 by Jericho Brown. Reprinted by permission of The Permissions Company, LLC on behalf of Copper Canyon Press (www.coppercanyonpress.org) and by permission of Macmillan Publishers International Ltd. on behalf of Picador.

"O Small Sad Ecstasy of Love" copyright © 2020 by Anne Carson. Originally published in *Poem-a-Day*. Reprinted by permission of the author and Aragi, Inc. All rights reserved.

"Broken Sestina Reaching for Black Joy" from *Scorched Earth*. Copyright © 2025 by Tiana Clark. Reprinted by permission of Washington Square Press/Atria Books, an imprint of Simon & Schuster, LLC. All rights reserved.

"1994" from *How to Carry Water: Selected Poems*. Copyright © 1996 by Lucille Clifton. Reprinted by permission of The Permissions Company, LLC on behalf of BOA Editions, Ltd., www.boaeditions.org. And from *Blessing the Boats* by Lucille Clifton published by Penguin Classics. Copyright © 2000 by Lucille Clifton. Reprinted by permission of Penguin Books Ltd.

"When I Left the King" from *Book of Mercy*. Copyright © 1984 by Leonard Cohen. Reprinted by permission of The Wylie Agency, LLC.

"To My Husband" from *Collected Poems*. Copyright © 2025 by Wendy Cope. Reprinted by permission of Faber & Faber, Ltd.

"Provision" from *Paper Cathedrals*. Copyright © 2001 by Morri Creech. Reprinted by permission of Kent State University Press.

"The Language" from *The Collected Poems of Robert Creeley 1945–1975*. Copyright © 1982 by The Regents of The University of California. Reprinted by permission of the University of California Press through PLSclear.

"Grief Work" from *Postcolonial Love Poem*. Copyright © 2020 by Natalie Diaz. Reprinted by permission of The Permissions Company, LLC on behalf of Graywolf Press (www.graywolfpress.org) and by permission of Faber & Faber, Ltd.

"The Strength of Fields" from *Poems 1957–1967*. Copyright © 1967 by James Dickey. Reprinted by permission of Wesleyan University Press.

"Canary" from *Grace Notes*. Copyright © 1989 by Rita Dove. Reprinted by permission of W. W. Norton & Company, Inc.

"Beauty" from *The Art of the Lathe*. Copyright © 1998 by B. H. Fairchild. Reprinted by permission of The Permissions Company, LLC on behalf of Alice James Books, www.alicejamesbooks.org.

"The Glory Façade" from *The Skin of Meaning*. Copyright © 2023 by Keith Flynn. Reprinted by permission of The Permissions Company, LLC on behalf of Red Hen Press, www.redhen.org.

"The Jungle" from *The Life*. Copyright © 2021 by Carrie Fountain. Reprinted by permission of Penguin Books, an imprint of Penguin Publishing Group, a division of Penguin Random House, LLC. All rights reserved.

"Taking It" from *Forest Primeval*. Copyright © 2016 by Vievee Francis. Reprinted by permission of TriQuarterly Books/Northwestern University Press. All rights reserved.

"A Small Needful Fact" and "Catalog of Unbashed Gratitude" from *Catalog of Unbashed Gratitude*. Copyright © 2015 by Ross Gay. Reprinted by permission of the University of Pittsburgh Press.

"The Forgotten Dialect of the Heart" from *The Great Fires: Poems 1982–1992*. Copyright © 1994 by Jack Gilbert. Reprinted by permission of Alfred A. Knopf, an imprint of the Knopf Doubleday Publishing Group, a division of Penguin Random House, LLC. All rights reserved.

"Kingdon Animalia" from *Kingdom Animalia*. Copyright © 2011 by Aracelis Girmay. Reprinted by permission of The Permissions Company, LLC on behalf of BOA Editions, Ltd., www.boaeditions.org.

"Archaic Fragment" from *Averno*. Copyright © 2006 by Louise Glück. Reprinted by permission of Farrar, Straus and Giroux and Carcanet Press. All rights reserved.

"Mother and Child (The Road at the Edge of the Field)" from *Place*. Copyright © 2012 by Jorie Graham. Reprinted by permission of HarperCollins Publishers.

"Etiology" from *All of It Singing: New and Selected Poems*. Copyright © 1999 by Linda Gregg. Reprinted by permission of The Permissions Company, LLC on behalf of Graywolf Press, www.graywolfpress.org.

"Theories of Revenge" copyright © 2021 by Paul Guest. Originally published in *The Missouri Review*. Reprinted by permission of the author.

"enough food and a mom" from *play dead*. Copyright © 2017 by francine j. harris. Reprinted by permission of The Permissions Company, LLC on behalf of Alice James Books, www.alicejamesbooks.org.

"Meditation at Lagunitas" from *Praise*. Copyright © 1979 by Robert Hass. Reprinted by permission of HarperCollins Publishers.

"Those Winter Sundays" from *Collected Poems of Robert Hayden*, edited by Frederick Glaysher. Copyright © 1966 by Robert Hayden. Reprinted by permission of Liveright Publishing Corporation.

"At Pegasus" from *Muscular Music*. Copyright © 2006 by Terrance Hayes. Reprinted by permissions of Tia Chucha Press.

"The Supple Deer" from *Come, Thief*. Copyright © 2011 by Jane Hirshfield. Reprinted by permission of Alfred A. Knopf, an imprint of the Knopf Doubleday Publishing Group, a division of Penguin Random House, LLC, and by permission of the author. All rights reserved.

"The Gift" from *The Jaguar*. Copyright © 2022 by Sarah Holland-Batt. Reprinted by permission of the University of Queensland Press.

"love & the memory of it" from *Still Life.* Copyright © 2024 by Jay Hopler. Reprinted by permission of McSweeney's Publishing.

"Part of Eve's Discussion" from *The Good Thief.* Copyright © 1988 by Marie Howe. Reprinted by permission of Persea Books, Inc. www.perseabooks.com. All rights reserved.

"Mummy of a Lady Named Jemutesonekh" from *Letters to a Stranger*. Copyright © 1973 by Thomas James. Reprinted by permission of HarperCollins Publishers.

"Now" from *The Throne of the Third Heaven of the Nations Millennium General Assembly.* Copyright © 1969, 1976, 1982, 1987, and 1995 by Denis Johnson. Reprinted by permission of HarperCollins Publishers.

"Author's Prayer" from *Dancing in Odessa*. Copyright © 2014 and 2021 by Ilya Kaminsky. Reprinted by permission of Tupelo Press and Faber and Faber, Ltd.

"Get Up, Please" from *Get Up, Please*. Copyright © 2016 by David Kirby. Reprinted by permission of Louisiana State University Press.

"Facing It" from *Pleasure Dome: New and Collected Poems*. Copyright © 2001 by Yusef Komunyakaa. Reprinted by permissions of Wesleyan University Press.

"The Layers" from *The Collected Poems*. Copyright © 1978 by Stanley Kunitz. Reprinted by permission of W. W. Norton & Company, Inc.

"Edible" from *Bonfire Opera*. Copyright © 2020 by Danusha Laméris. Reprinted by permission of The University of Pittsburgh Press.

"From Blossoms" from *Rose*. Copyright © 1986 by Li-Young Lee. Reprinted by permission of The Permissions Company, LLC on behalf of BOA Editions, Ltd., www.boaeditions.org.

"Winter Stars" from *Winter Stars*. Copyright © 1985 by Larry Levis. Reprinted by permission of the University of Pittsburgh Press.

"You Can Take Off Your Sweater" from *Space Struck*. Copyright © 2019 by Paige Lewis. Reprinted by permission of The Permissions Company, LLC on behalf of Sarabande Books, www.sarabandebooks.org.

"And I Was Alive" from *Stolen Air: Selected Poems of Osip Mandelstam*, selected and translated by Christian Wiman. Copyright © 2012 by Christian Wiman. Reprinted by permission of HarperCollins Publishers.

"Willful" from *White Sea*. Copyright © 2008 by Cleopatra Mathis. Reprinted by permission of The Permissions Company, LLC on behalf of Sarabande Books, www.sarabandebooks.org.

"Mingus in Diaspora" from *Search Party: Collected Poems of William Matthews*. Copyright © 2004 by Sebastian Matthews and Stanley Plumly. Reprinted by permission of HarperCollins Publishers.

"The Ferry" from *Previously Owned*. Copyright © 2022 by Nathan McClain. Reprinted by permission of The Permissions Company, LLC on behalf of Four Way Books, www.fourwaybooks.com.

"Vixen" from *The Vixen*. Copyright © 1995 by W. S. Merwin. Reprinted by permission of Alfred A. Knopf, an imprint of the Knopf Doubleday Publishing Group, a division of Penguin Random House, LLC. All rights reserved.

"Black Site (Exhibit I)" from *Sand Opera*. Copyright © 2015 by Philip Metres. Reprinted by permission of The Permissions Company, LLC on behalf of Alice James Books, www.alicejamesbooks.org.

"Encounter" from *The Collected Poems 1931–1987*. Copyright © 1988 by Czesław Miłosz Royalties, Inc. Reprinted by permission of HarperCollins Publishers.

"Sleeping with the Dictionary" from *Sleeping with the Dictionary*. Copyright © 2002 by Harryette Mullen. Reprinted by permission of the University of California Press.

"Upon Reading that Eric Dolphy Transcribed Even the Calls of Certain Species of Birds" from *Kontemporary Amerikan Poetry*. Copyright © 2020 by John Murillo. Reprinted by permission of The Permissions Company, LLC on behalf of Four Way Books, www.fourwaybooks.com.

"Conjoined Twins" from *Two Worlds Exist*. Copyright © 2016 by Yehoshua November. Reprinted by permission of Orison Books, Inc. All rights reserved.

"Full Summer" from *Wellspring*. Copyright © 1996 by Sharon Olds. Reprinted by permission of Alfred A. Knopf, an imprint of the Knopf Doubleday Publishing Group, a division of Penguin Random House, LLC. All rights reserved.

"Nate Brown Is Looking for a Moose" from *Contradictions in the Design*. Copyright © 2016 by Matthew Olzmann. Reprinted by permission of The Permissions Company, LLC on behalf of Alice James Books, www.alicejamesbooks.org.

"The Burning of Giordano Bruno" from *Obscura*. Copyright © 2020 by Frank Paino. Reprinted by permission of Orison Books, Inc. All rights reserved.

"Search for the New Land" copyright © 2019 by Morgan Parker. Originally published in *The New York Review of Books.* Reprinted by permission of the author.

"Ethics" from *Waiting for My Life*. Copyright © 1981 by Linda Pastan. Reprinted by permission of W. W. Norton & Company, Inc. and The Estate of Linda Pastan in care of the Jean V. Naggar Literary Agency, Inc.

"Song" from *Song*. Copyright © 1995 by Brigit Pegeen Kelly. Reprinted by permission of The Permissions Company, LLC on behalf of BOA Editions, Ltd., www.boaeditions.org.

"In a Low Voice, Slowly" from *Then The War and Selected Poems 2007–2020*. Copyright © 2022 by Carl Phillips. Reprinted by permission of Farrar, Straus and Giroux and Carcanet Press. All rights reserved.

"ICU" from *The Road to Emmaus*. Copyright © 2014 by Spencer Reece. Reprinted by permission of Farrar, Straus and Giroux. All rights reserved.

"Lost Body" from *Constellarium*. Copyright © 2016 by Jordan Rice. Reprinted by permission of Orison Books, Inc. All rights reserved.

"Men's Sexual-Trauma Support Group" copyright © 2024 by José Antonio Rodríguez. Originally published in *The New Yorker*. Reprinted by permission of the author.

"Buen Esqueleto" from *Lima :: Limón*. Copyright © 2019 by Natalie Scenters-Zapico. Reprinted by permission of The Permissions Company, LLC on behalf of Copper Canyon Press, www.coppercanyonpress.org.

"Object Permanence" from *Ordinary Beast*. Copyright © 2017 by Nicole Sealey. Reprinted by permission of HarperCollins Publishers.

"High Romance" from *Modern Poetry*. Copyright © 2024 by Diane Seuss. Reprinted by permission of The Permissions Company, LLC on behalf of Graywolf Press (www.graywolfpress.org) and by permission of Fitzcarraldo Editions.

"Trace Evidence" from *Trace Evidence*. Copyright © 2023 by Charif Shanahan. Reprinted by permission of Tin House, an imprint of Zando, LLC, and by permission of the author.

"Scheherazade" from *Crush*. Copyright © 2005 by Richard Siken. Reprinted by permission of Yale University Press.

"Alternate Names for Black Boys" from *[INSERT] BOY.* Copyright © 2014 by Danez Smith. Reprinted by permission of YesYes Books.

"Good Bones" from *Good Bones*. Copyright © 2017 by Maggie Smith. Reprinted by permission of The Permissions Company, LLC, on behalf of Tupelo Press, www.tupelopress.org.

"Wade in the Water" from *Such Color: New and Selected Poems*. Copyright © 2018 by Tracy K. Smith. Reprinted by permission of The Permissions Company, LLC on behalf of Graywolf Press, www.graywolfpress.org.

"Ask Me" from *Ask Me: 100 Essential Poems*. Copyright © 1977 and 2014 by William Stafford and the Estate of William Stafford. Reprinted by permission of The Permissions Company, LLC on behalf of Graywolf Press, www.graywolfpress.org.

"Metamorphosis" from *What Love Comes To: New and Selected Poems*. Copyright © 1971 and 2011 by Ruth Stone. Reprinted by permission of The Permissions Company, LLC on behalf of Copper Canyon Press, www.coppercanyonpress.org.

"Stairs and Windows" copyright © 2023 by Cole Swenson. Originally published in *Big Other*. Reprinted by permission of the author.

"Psalm" from *Map: Collected and Last Poems by Wisława Szymborska*. Translated by Clare Cavanagh and Stanisław Barańczak. All works by Wisława Szymborska copyright © The Wisława Szymborska Foundation. English translation copyright © 2015 by HarperCollins Publishers. Reprinted by permission of HarperCollins Publishers.

"Threshold" from *Selected Poems 1946–1968*. Copyright © 1986 by R. S. Thomas. Reprinted by permission of Bloodaxe Books.

"In the War: you and houses" from *Things You May Find Hidden in My Ear: Poems from Gaza*. Copyright © 2022 by Mosab Abu Toha. Reprinted by permission of The Permissions Company, LLC on behalf of City Lights Books, www.citylights.com.

"Incident" from *Native Guard*. Copyright © 2006 by Natasha Trethewey. Reprinted by permission of HarperCollins Publishers.

"Door in the Mountain" from *Door in the Mountain*. Copyright © 2004 by Jean Valentine. Reprinted by permission of Wesleyan University Press.

"Telemachus" from *Night Sky with Exit Wounds*. Copyright © 2016 and 2017 by Ocean Vuong. Reprinted by permission of The Permissions Company, LLC on behalf of Copper Canyon Press (www.coppercanyonpress.org) and by permission of The Random House Group, Ltd. on behalf of Jonathan Cape.

"Quae Nocent Saepe Docent" from *Charm Offensive*. Copyright © 2023 by Ross White. Reprinted by permission of Eyewear Publishing, Ltd.

"Love's Last" from *Once in the West*. Copyright © 2014 by Christian Wiman. Reprinted by permission of Farrar, Straus and Giroux. All rights reserved.

About the Editors

Luke Hankins is the author of the poetry collections *MAGNITUDE: New & Selected Poems* (TRP, 2027), *Radiant Obstacles*, and *Weak Devotions*, as well as a poetry chapbook, *Testament*. He is also the author of a collection of essays, *The Work of Creation*, and a volume of translations from the French of Stella Vinitchi Radulescu, *A Cry in the Snow & Other Poems*. With Nomi Stone, Hankins is co-editor of *Between Paradise & Earth: Eve Poems*. He is the founder and editor of Orison Books, a non-profit literary press focused on the life of the spirit from a broad and inclusive range of perspectives.

Poet and anthropologist **Nomi Stone** is the author of three books, most recently the poetry collection *Kill Class* (Tupelo, 2019), finalist for the Julie Suk Award, and the ethnography *Pinelandia: An Anthropology and Field Poetics of War and Empire* (University of California Press, 2023), first prize in the Middle East Studies Award from the American Anthropological Association and Honorable Mention of the Middle East Studies Association's Albert Hourani Prize. With Luke Hankins, Stone is co-editor of *Between Paradise & Earth: Eve Poems*. Winner of a Pushcart Prize and a Fulbright fellowship, she was most recently a Postdoctoral Researcher in Anthropology at Princeton and she is currently an Associate Professor of Poetry at the University of Texas, Dallas.